THE GREAT CENTRAL CANADA BUCKET LIST

ROBIN ESROCK

ONE -OF-A- KIND TRAVEL EXPERIENCES

DUNDURN
TORONTO

For Bradley and Staci Kalmek

Library and Archives Canada Cataloguing in Publication
Esrock, Robin, 1974-, author

The great Central Canada bucket list : one-of-a-kind travel experiences / Robin Esrock.

Issued in print and electronic formats.
ISBN 978-1-4597-2968-1 (pbk.).--ISBN 978-1-4597-2969-8 (pdf).--
ISBN 978-1-4597-2970-4 (epub)

1. Ontario--Guidebooks. 2. Québec (Province)--Guidebooks. 3. Esrock, Robin, 1974- --Travel--Ontario. 4. Esrock, Robin, 1974- -- Travel--Québec (Province). 5. Ontario--Description and travel. 6. Québec (Province)--Description and travel. I. Title.

FC3057.E86 2015   917.1304'5   C2014-907091-8
                                                      C2014-907092-6

Editor: Allison Hirst
Cover and text concept: Tania Craan
Cover design: Courtney Horner
Text design: Laura Boyle
Cover images: Thinkstock; Robin Esrock; Robin Esrock; Courtesy Edgewalk CN Tower; Éliane Excoffier; Au Pied de Cochon; Robin Esrock; Robin Esrock (back)

  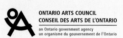

1   2   3   4   5   19   18   17   16   15
We acknowledge the support of the **Canada Council for the Arts** and the **Ontario Arts Council** for our publishing program. We also acknowledge the financial support of the **Government of Canada** through the **Canada Book Fund** and **Livres Canada Books**, and the **Government of Ontario** through the **Ontario Book Publishing Tax Credit** and the **Ontario Media Development Corporation**.

Care has been taken to trace the ownership of copyright material used in this book. The author and the publisher welcome any information enabling them to rectify any references or credits in subsequent editions.

J. Kirk Howard, President

The publisher is not responsible for websites or their content unless they are owned by the publisher.

Printed and bound in Canada.

Visit us at
Dundurn.com | @dundurnpress | Facebook.com/dundurnpress | Pinterest.com/dundurnpress

Dundurn
3 Church Street, Suite 500
Toronto, Ontario, Canada
M5E 1M2

CONTENTS

INTRODUCTION

There once was an Upper Canada, and a Lower Canada. One was stupendously English, the other French, *bien sûr!* Backed by the duelling powers of Britain and France, the two Canadas were at odds, for despite their Upper and Lower designation, both wanted to be on top. Fortunately, they realized that neither needed a foreign master, especially when they had each other. With vast political and economic power, the top and bottom of Canada consummated to create an idea that ultimately attracted provinces from further afield, resulting in a magnificent, *merveilleux* country, simply named Canada. One hundred and fifty years later, Ontario (Upper Canada) and Quebec (Lower Canada) remain the beating heart of the nation. Like a married couple, they've had their ups and downs, but have somehow battled through it to everyone's mutual advantage. There is blessedly little deep-seated provincial rivalry, other than hockey games and backroom snickers; political bickering, sure, but an inspirational example of what can be accomplished if two cultures, languages, and histories join together.

While there are facts aplenty in these pages, this is not a book about the history of Central Canada. Instead, you're holding a personal investigation into some of the finest travel experiences Ontario and Quebec have to offer. Here I have written about places to visit and things to do that you simply cannot do anywhere else in the world. I know this because I spent ten years travelling to over one hundred countries across the globe in search of bucket list experiences. I wrote about them as a columnist for newspapers and magazines, and showcased them as a host for an internationally syndicated television show. Returning home after each adventure abroad, I became increasingly curious about the bucket list experiences in my own backyard. Two years, ten provinces, and three

territories later, I concluded that Canada's backyard is too big to even call a backyard. I have also realized that Canada, and in particular Ontario and Quebec, is far weirder and more wonderful than most people think.

Nowhere else in the world can you slam yourself harmlessly against a red-rock coastline, skate (or attempt to, anyway) on the world's largest skating rink, party in an ice castle at the world's biggest winter festival, explore a temple of hockey, or eat poutine laced with foie gras. All one-of-a-kind experiences — spanning adventure, culture, history, and food. I even managed to fit in overnight stays in two very unique accommodations: a haunted prison cell *and* an ice hotel.

Bucket lists are as different as the people who create them, but my selection criteria were simple: Is it unique to Canada? Can anyone and everyone do it? Is this something you'll remember for the rest of your life? Tick all three boxes, and it made my shortlist. Some of these experiences are pricey; others are as free as the jazz performances in Montreal's Place des Festivals. While you may have found this book in the guidebook section, *The Great Central Canada Bucket List*, like other books in the series, is less about *information* and more about *inspiration*. Updated practical tips and more detailed information can be found on the extensive companion website I built to accompany each experience.

Ontarians and Quebeckers will recognize many of these experiences, perhaps without really knowing them. Canadian and international visitors will enjoy discovering the highlights of the region. Armchair travellers can follow the journey of an immigrant — who happens to make his living travelling the world — discovering the rich bounty of experiences at home. Are there omissions? Certainly. Healthy bucket lists evolve with the people who write them. As I continue to travel across Canada, I'm listening, learning, and continuing to expand the *Great Canadian Bucket List*.

Home to 60 percent of the country's population, Ontario and Quebec often feel like two different countries. During the course of my journey, Canada itself felt like thirteen countries wrapped in one border, which made for particularly rewarding travel. For locals who don't know where to begin ticking off their bucket lists, simply start with what's close by. For those visiting through the international portals of Toronto or Montreal, here are the remarkable experiences you have been looking for.

Once upon a time, there was Ontario and there was Quebec. One was stupendously English, the other French, *bien sûr!* And as you'll learn in these pages, the two provinces that make up Central Canada today are fun, *fantastique*, and full of bucket list–worthy inspiration.

Robin Esrock
Vancouver, B.C.

USING THIS BOOK

You will notice this book includes little information about prices, where to stay, where to eat, the best time to go and what you should pack. Important stuff certainly, but practicalities that shift and change with far more regularity than print editions of a book. With this in mind, I've created online and social media channels to accompany the inspirational guide you hold in your hands. Here you will find all the information noted above, along with videos, galleries, reading guides and more.

By visiting www.canadianbucketlist.com, you can also join our community of bucket listers, find exclusive discounts for many of the activities discussed in this book, win prizes, and debate the merits of these and other experiences. When you register, unlock the entire site by entering the code BUCK3TL15T, or access each item individually with the START HERE link at the end of each chapter.

DISCLAIMER

Tourism is a constantly changing business. Hotels may change names, restaurants may change owners and some activities may no longer be available at all. Records fall and facts shift. While the utmost care has been taken to ensure the information provided is accurate, the author and publisher take no responsibility for errors, or for any incidents that might occur in your pursuit of these activities.

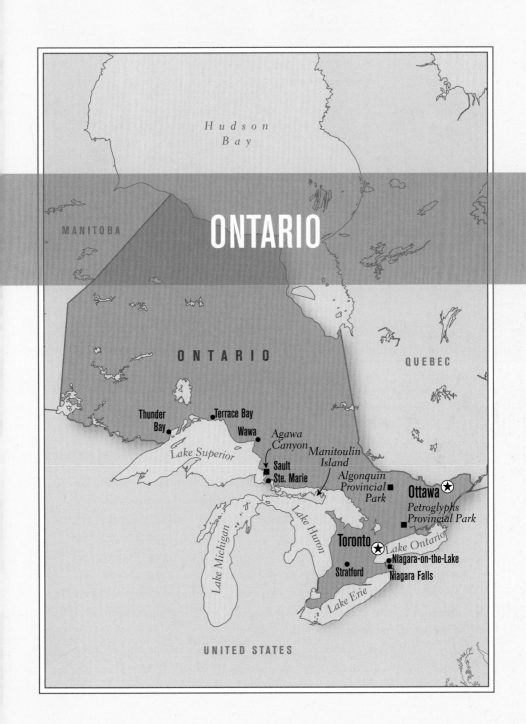

ONTARIO

Hudson
Bay

MANITOBA

ONTARIO

QUEBEC

Thunder
Bay

Terrace Bay

Wawa

Agawa
Canyon

Manitoulin
Island

Sault
Ste. Marie

Algonquin
Provincial
Park

Ottawa

Petroglyphs
Provincial Park

Lake Superior

Lake Michigan

Lake Huron

Toronto

Lake Ontario

Niagara-on-the-Lake

Stratford

Niagara Falls

Lake Erie

UNITED STATES

SPEND A NIGHT IN JAIL

On a personal list of dubious achievements, being incarcerated for something silly does have a certain appeal. Perhaps it shows that even honourable, noble lives have roguish moments. Perhaps it's because one night of prison reaffirms the benefits of freedom. Perhaps it's just something interesting to say at a dinner party, provided the words "misunderstanding," "no criminal record" and "that was an adventure!" are used in the story. Of course, the reality of prison is entirely devoid of charm. There's nothing fun about being locked away in an institutional cell, denied the joys of modern life, surrounded by people who actually deserve to be there. Still, our Bucket List demands adventurous transgressions, and fortunately I found a prison cell where I could leave with my reputation, and clean criminal record, healthily intact.

"When they chained up the naked prisoners on the cement floor in pure darkness, were they on their backs?" This is the kind of detail that arrests my curiosity as I stand outside the "Hole" cells

in the basement of the HI-Ottawa Jail Youth Hostel. For 110 years, the thick-stoned building on Nicholas Street was known as the Carleton County Gaol, an imposing hell designed to imprison the city's most notorious offenders. Built in 1862 as a "model" British prison, the reality was far less respectable: tiny cells crammed with both men and boys (as young as five years old), reeking of excrement, the floor crawling with bugs and rats. The Gaol was eventually shut down in 1972 due to inhumane living conditions, but it reopened the following year as a refurbished youth hostel. The new owners clearly knew the lengths backpackers will go to save a buck. Today, budget travellers spend the night bunking in the original cells, drink beer in the canteen that once fed prisoners slop, and wake in fear with blood-drained ghosts hovering over their beds.

Okay, I made the ghosts part up, but just barely. Ghost Walks Ottawa holds nightly prison tours in the old jail, guiding the public and hostel guests to some of the original, unrestored sections of the prison, recounting trials and tales, and revealing why this has been called one of the world's most haunted buildings. After touring the punishment cells, my Ghost Walks guide, Adriane, leads me to the eighth floor, still in its original state. The cells are punishingly small. She paints a vivid picture of life for a nineteenth-century prisoner and explains the sad, short life of Patrick J. Whelan, the man who murdered Thomas D'Arcy McGee, one of the Fathers of Confederation. Whelan met his maker at the jail during the last public execution in Canada. I'm led to

the actual gallows, thoughtfully decorated with a hangman's rope. Five thousand people desperate for entertainment watched Whelan squirm for ten minutes. Even though Adriane has been guiding tours in the old jail for over a year, she's edgy and freaked-out as we wander through Death Row. She nervously tells me about doors slamming, disembodied voices, guests reporting ghosts at the edge of their bunks. Seriously!

I bid her adieu, retire to my cell, slam the iron bars shut, and make sure it's locked from the inside. Lying in my bed, I try not to think about the poor, miserable bastards who rotted away in Cell 4. It's deathly quiet, save for the snoring of someone in an adjacent cell. Although the walls are thick, the vaulted ceilings were designed to carry sound so guards could hear even the faintest of

whispers. I somehow fall asleep, but wake up in a cold sweat at four a.m. Worse, I need to pee, which means I have to leave the safety of my cell and walk down the long, dark hallway. At the point of bursting, I muster the courage to rise and walk to the bathroom, but decide to film the whole thing, just in case I become the first guy to catch a ghost on camera. Relieved, I return to my cell, toss and turn for hours, and thank God, Jesus, Buddha, Allah, and Elvis that I'm a free man, condemned to spend but one night in Canada's only prison hotel.

START HERE: canadianbucketlist.com/jail

ONTARIO

5

PAY YOUR RESPECTS

Several readers will feel that celebrating Canada Day on Parliament Hill is an experience that belongs on the nation's bucket list. Touring Parliament might be another, and I'm not one to argue. The building itself is as grand as any of the great halls of power. With its imposing Peace Tower punctuating the sky like an exclamation mark, Parliament is a landmark that oozes grandeur. I personally found the most moving spectacle in the capital to be Remembrance Day, taking place each November 11. It's a solemn affair, brightened only by flowered wreaths and red plastic poppies pinned on jacket lapels. Aging Canadian veterans parade downtown to the National War Memorial, where they meet the prime minister, the governor general, and a Silver Cross Mother — a woman who has lost her son in battle. Wreaths are placed at the steps of the memorial, a children's choir sings, and, if the weather permits, Royal Canadian Air Force jets crackle across the sky.

I watch as a Second World War veteran, motivated by the power of his memories, stands up from his wheelchair and marches forward proudly, exhausting hidden stores of energy. The haunting bugler plays "Taps," signifying the last call, and the sound echoes off the surrounding buildings. Thousands of people — soldiers, veterans, locals, and tourists — line the streets, showing quiet respect. At exactly 11:00 a.m., a sunbeam pierces through a single window in the Canadian War Museum's Memorial Hall, illuminating the headstone of the grave of Canada's Unknown Soldier. This is powerful stuff: a moving reminder of so many young lights extinguished before they had the opportunity to tick off their own bucket lists. An important reminder of how fortunate we are to be able to tick off our own.

START HERE: www.canadianbucketlist.com/remembrance

VISIT THE HOCKEY HALL OF FAME

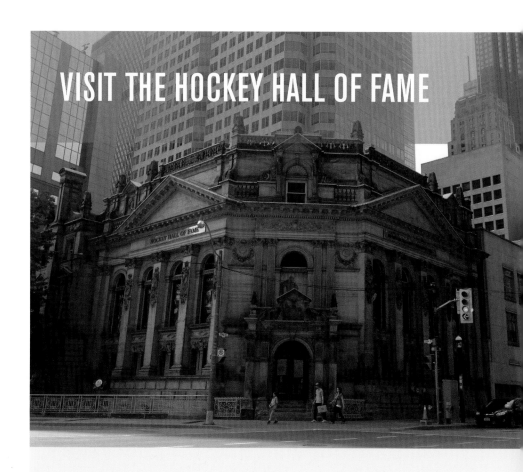

"Please, for the love of God, can someone explain to me what's going on?"

It's my first week as an immigrant in Canada, and I'm staring at a TV set broadcasting twelve millionaires on ice skates. My older brother, who moved to Canada a few years before I did, has already forgotten our childhood sports of cricket, rugby, and soccer, and is now wearing a Vancouver Canucks hockey vest. His conversion to Canada's national religion took less than a year, but my love for cricket bats and rugby balls will not allow me to yield quite as easily. First, how can anyone take seriously a team called the Canucks? Blackhawks, Predators, Sharks, Devils, Flames — those are some badass-sounding teams. But Canucks? Canadiens?

Senators? Maple Leafs? Oooh, I'm trembling. Second, hockey to the uninitiated is too fast to watch, too difficult to understand, and too painful to listen to, especially when a guy named Don Cherry gets on his soapbox. Further, the fact that I skate like an ostrich on Rollerblades clouds my understanding of the skills and talent needed to distinguish oneself in the National Hockey League. I'm not proud of it, but when I arrived in Canada, a Puck was a character from Shakespeare.

During the regular season, when it felt as if the Canucks played a game twice a day, I never quite got what all the hubbub was about . . . until I visited the Hockey Hall of Fame. Standing on the corner of Yonge and Front in downtown Toronto, the HHOF is located in what was once a Bank of Montreal office, a grand-looking building sculpted with gravity and pomp. To get inside, you have to walk through a shopping mall, which may be symbolic of the commercialization of the sport, or a practical way to control the daily crowds. And they come from far and wide, these worshippers of the vulcanized rubber puck, ready to open their wallets and drop their jaws at exhibits of the game's great knights, and stand before the Holy Grail itself: Lord Stanley's Cup.

With sixteen different exhibits, I'm not sure where to start, so I head to the Hartland Molson Theatre to watch an introductory movie.

Canada's Official Sports

The unusual contradiction that Canada's most wildly popular sport wasn't its official national pastime was finally laid to rest in 1994. Up until that point, a game originating with Algonquin tribes along the St. Lawrence Valley was Canada's official game. In fact, lacrosse was the country's most popular sport until hockey usurped it around 1900. When politicians sought to resolve the situation, they agreed on a compromise whereby lacrosse became Canada's national summer game and hockey its national winter game. Any attempt to play either sport typically leaves me sprawled out in a bloody pulp. ➤

ONTARIO ↑

If you edited the most stirring scenes from *Rocky*, *Hoosiers*, and *The Natural* with *Gladiator* and *Braveheart*, you might approach the spirit of this sweeping, epic journey through Canada's great game. A frozen pond, wooden sticks, men with pencil-thin moustaches, and the recipe for legends. The film explains the development of the game, the teams, the rules, and culminates in the quest for the Stanley Cup.

I leave the theatre inspired to learn more, to meet the heroes of the game: Cyclone Taylor, Ken Dryden, Gordie Howe, Bobbie Orr, Mario Lemieux, and a goal machine they call simply The Great One. After the exhibits in the NHL Zone, I wander over to the scale replica of the Canadiens' dressing room from the Montreal Forum. It's the first time I hold a stick and feel the weight of a puck in my palm. In the Dynasties exhibit, I learn about the dominance and

great rivalry of the Canadiens and the Maple Leafs from the 1950s to the late 1970s, the emergence of the Oilers, and the dearth of Canadian domination ever since. In a large section called the World of Hockey, I'm amazed to see that the game extends beyond just northern countries to teams in Australia, Turkey, Mongolia, and, yes, even my old South Africa. Women play hockey, kids play hockey . . . I leave the exhibits knowing the world is hockey mad, with Canadians the maddest of all.

The Great Hall of NHL trophies is approached with reverence. Here are the game's most sought-after pieces of silverware, including the original bowl donated by Governor General Lord Stanley, and the Stanley Cup itself. I'm told it's the hardest trophy to win in world sports, but fortunately it's easy enough to stand next to and get someone to take a snapshot. Finally, I'm drawn to the interactive section of the HHOF. The Be-A-Player Zone allows me to put on some kit and play the goalie in a life-sized net. In the Slapshot Zone, I learn that shooting is difficult enough, never mind scoring. In the Broadcast Zone, I give a live play-by-play of a recorded game, then convince a kid to play some table hockey.

By the time I leave the Hall of Fame, my conversion to Canada's national religion is complete. It's game night, and the Habs are playing the Canucks. I head over to a bar, order a pint, and, for the first time, anticipate where the puck will go, understand how the rules work, and thrill at just how big the hits can be. A tourist innocently wanders in front of me.

"For the love of God, move outta the way, I'm trying to watch the game!"

START HERE: canadianbucketlist.com/hhof

AVOID NUCLEAR ARMAGEDDON

You haven't lived until you've seen just how close we all came to dying. About thirty kilometres outside Ottawa is a bone-chilling, fascinating, and entirely unique glimpse into a time when geopolitics tightroped along a knife's edge. Two superpowers were headlocked in a Cold War, armed with atomic and hydrogen bombs capable of wiping entire cities off the map and poisoning anyone lucky enough to survive the nuclear Armageddon. Canada recognized that the end might indeed be nigh and set to work on a top-secret military bunker that would ensure the survival of its government. Commissioned by Prime Minister John Diefenbaker, 9,300 square metres of Ontario countryside were excavated to make room for a four-storey-deep underground fortress, using 5,000 tons of steel, 25,000 cubic metres of concrete, and $22 million of 1960's taxpayer dollars.

The Diefenbunker, as it became known, was a full-service facility in which 535 lucky bureaucrats would have the task of somehow rebuilding whatever was left of Canada. These appointees were selected based on their profession, not their personal qualifications.

ONTARIO

How I Learned to Worry and Fear the Bomb

A visit to the Diefenbunker wasn't my first exposure to the highly niche world of atomic tourism. In Ukraine, I visited a former top-secret nuclear missile base and was given a tour of its underground control station by a former Soviet general who once had his finger on the button. Men like him were trained — and carefully monitored — to destroy the entire planet on an order. Several times in history, that order was almost given, typically as the result of a computer glitch. In Canada, Prime Minister John Diefenbaker authorized the construction of fifty Emergency Government Headquarters around the country. Smaller regional "Diefenbunkers" were built in Nanaimo (BC), Penhold (AB), Shilo (MB), Borden (ON), Valcartier (QC) and Debert (NS), along with other communication sites. While some are still active military installations, most were sold off or destroyed. ➤

No family members were included, and, rather naively, no psychological considerations were taken into account. A large group of mostly men would emerge weeks later into a world of ashes and radioactive zombies. These, apparently, would be the lucky ones.

Fortunately, none of this happened. Despite several near misses (you know about the Cuban Missile Crisis, and you might want to search Able Archer), the Iron Curtain smelted, the world evolved, and children no longer have to memorize how to duck and cover under a fireball. The Diefenbunker functioned as a military telecommunications base until the 1990s, at which time it was decommissioned and turned into a Cold War museum. Due to the increasing sophistication of nuclear weapons, there simply wouldn't be time today to relocate government to the base, and at no time was the Diefenbunker used for its intended purpose. The only PM to actually visit the base was Pierre Trudeau, who promptly cut its operating budget.

Today, anyone can enter the 115-metre-long blast tunnel, cross through intimidating 36-centimetre-thick bank vault doors, and explore the fully equipped world below. I'm greeted by Mike Braham, the former director of Emergency Preparedness Canada and now an enthusiastic volunteer at the museum. Mike was one of those chosen to survive in the Emergency Government Situation Centre. Shaking his head in disbelief, he reckons the real victims would have

been the ones trapped inside the bunker. "With no psychological preparedness, these people would have gone nuts," he tells me.

The bunker was designed to withstand a five-megaton blast up to a couple of kilometres away. That's 250 times more powerful than Hiroshima. Its air would be triple filtered and, in theory at least, supplies would last up to thirty days. "People couldn't see beyond thirty days of nuclear war," explains Mike.

He leads me through the decontamination area and the medical and dental centres that have been transformed into excellent Cold War exhibitions. School kids might giggle at relics such as rotary phones and 1.5-metre-high computers. Adults have an entirely different reaction. "We came close, but we felt, we hoped, that common sense would prevail," says Mike.

I sit at the prime minister's desk, peering at his mounted toilet, and learn about the escape hatch, canteen, and Bank of Canada vault. Today, the Diefenbunker hosts parties, spy programs for kids, and even shows spy-era movies in a theatre. Hollywood has used its facilities, and the nearby small town of Carp has benefited from the tourism. Other bunkers around Canada have been destroyed, but much larger and still-operational facilities exist in the U.S. and Russia. We may live in a safer world, but as long as we possess the tools of our own destruction, the threat of Armageddon will always exist. For its unfiltered, radiation-free fresh air of much-needed perspective, the Diefenbunker is one for the bucket list.

START HERE: canadianbucketlist.com/diefenbunker

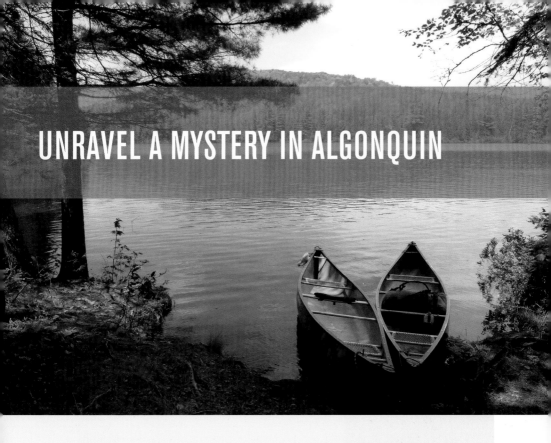

UNRAVEL A MYSTERY IN ALGONQUIN

Algonquin Park's rugged beauty has inspired an art movement, a mystery, countless wilderness adventures, and a sure-fire hit on the nation's bucket list. Quite an achievement considering Canada's oldest provincial park lacks the gee-whiz landscape of the Rockies, or the windswept vistas of the coasts. With all the tenacity of a black fly, Algonquin's beauty burrows under the skin, seducing visitors by demanding that they, too, must burrow inward — no motorized boats, no planes or cars. In this park of 2,500 lakes, one enters the realm of the canoe, one of the First Nations' best gifts to the world. The canoe is a technology so perfect that European explorers ditched their boats and took up the paddle as is. Our bucket list wants us to pick up the paddle, too.

After a four-hour drive north from Toronto, I enter Algonquin's Access Point #1: the park's 7,630 square kilometres of wilderness can be accessed via twenty-nine access points, your entry to 1,500 kilometres of canoe routes. On Canoe Lake, the park's busiest access point, wilderness lodges and fishing outfitters have done a roaring

ONTARIO

Howl at the Wolves

In the park's earliest days, Algonquin authorities set out to exterminate bears and wolves. After all, you can't have predators ruining an uptight, civilized Canadian's day in the park, can you? Fortunately, the hunters failed in their task and, ironically, Algonquin's more than thirty resident wolf packs are today one of the park's star attractions.

Each Thursday in August and September (until Labour Day), Algonquin Provincial Park hosts an unusual sing-along. More than five hundred cars line the side of Highway 60 for a public wolf howl. After a presentation about the wild Eastern wolves found in the park, naturalist staff lead the procession to a location with the best chance of success, instructing participants in the art of wolf howling. The humans call; the wolves respond. Wind, rain, and other factors can dampen the evening, but 1,500 people howling into the Algonquin darkness is worth the free admission. Arrive early, dress warmly, and make sure your gas tank is full. ➤

trade for over a century, but I've arrived in early June, with the busy season yet to kick into gear. Voyageur Quest has guided visitors into Algonquin from the northern Access # 1 for more than twenty-five years. They're happy to take me — a complete canoe newbie — several portages deep to Craig Lake. I don't know the correct way to hold a paddle, and my sixty-seven-year-old dad — a man who has never gone camping before, or even slept in a tent — is my canoeing companion. Adding further spice to the adventure pot is the fact that it is peak Bug Season, with a capital B. Bucket lists seldom shy away from taking one outside one's comfort zone, although I'm sure there are readers who have camped their entire lives, can start a fire by rubbing their fingers together, set up a tarp with the power of thought, and tie knots with the dexterity of a surgeon. I'm determined to prove a canoe trip in Algonquin is for *everybody*, although

it certainly helps to have one of those outdoorsy fellas handy, someone like our affable guide Matt Rothwell. He's got that gleam in his eye that shows that he is truly in love with the bush, and the demeanour of a welcoming host. Matt demonstrates the canoeing basics for us at Voyageur Quest's outfitting shop: the paddler up front provides the power, drawing forward, inward, or cross-bow drawing away. Paddler in the rear steers with movements called prying or sweeping. Canoes are surprisingly stable and can carry a lot of gear. Voyageurs — those hard-as-tack toughs who blazed the trail into Canada's interior — paddled up to twelve hours each day, carrying as much as two tons of supplies in their canoes.

We gather our tents, sleeping bags, food, and cooking gear, and it's all packed into waterproof bags and centred in the canoe. We'll need just two sets of clothes: one for paddling (which might get wet) and one for camp (which should remain dry). Crucial to the success of our mission is the following: bug jackets, bug dope, hats, cameras, sun block, rainwear, comfortable sandals, and twelve-year-old Glenfiddich. It also helps to have some background on Algonquin's most famous explorer, Tom Thomson.

Largely credited with inspiring the birth of Canada's greatest art movement, Thomson was a park ranger and guide who often disappeared into the thicket with his canoe, emerging days later with paintings and sketches that not only illustrated the park's natu-

↑

ONTARIO

ral magic but sparked the imagination of what would become the Group of Seven. These seven artists put Canada on the global art map, restlessly breaking from European tradition to capture a true north aesthetic. It was Thomson who introduced them to Algonquin, and it was Thomson who drowned in Canoe Lake under mysterious circumstances. His death, which preceded the formation of the Group of Seven, has spawned books, films, and no shortage of conspiracy theories.

"Look, there's no question about it. Thompson was murdered by Shannon Fraser, with a paddle … or maybe a candlestick, in the basement, dressed as a butler," I tell Matt over the fire. Flames are licking a pot sitting on the burning wood, a strong wind sending firebug-like sparks into the early evening sky and blessedly blowing the biting bugs away.

"I rather think it would have been wiser to have taken the ten most prominent Canadians and sunk them in Canoe Lake — and saved Tom Thomson."
– artist David Milne, in a letter to the National Gallery of Canada

Algonquin is comprised of a seemingly endless string of lakes, and our first day had consisted of several paddles and portages. For those unfamiliar, portaging involves balancing a canoe on your shoulders and hiking with it across land to the next put-in location (it also involves a return trip to pack in the rest of the gear). Canoes are designed for just such a task, and well-maintained portage trails are wide enough to accommodate them. I quickly got the hang of it, discovering that canoes make great echo chambers to sing motivational songs when traipsing through the forest. Each portage took us farther and farther away from civilization, deeper into the wilderness,

deeper into the joys and challenges of canoeing. We felt as if we had earned our lakeside campsite, the cool swim in the drinkable tea-brown water, Matt's fabulous spicy-chicken pasta dinner, and one of the most gorgeous sunsets I've ever seen. A storm front rolled past, leaving in its wake the kind of starry night where the Milky Way drips its dust all over you. My father is somewhat bewildered by his first night camping in the woods. He says *magnificent* a lot. A pair of loons yodels their distinctive call, and it might just be the wind, but we're convinced the wolves of Algonquin are howling their approval, too.

Voyageur Quest's customers typically opt for a three-day canoe trip, pampered by guides like Matt, with his honed campfire cooking skills (fresh bruschetta, salmon wraps, apple crumble, vegetable stir-fry, and gourmet sandwiches) and knack for story-telling, including Native legends surrounding the stars, trees, and fire. When the wind chill settles in, Matt promptly builds a makeshift sweat lodge around some of the hot rocks, steamed with water and soothing cedar leaves. If only every outdoor experience had a Matt.

After a sunrise paddle that serves up a muscular bull moose munching on lilies, we pack up camp and float to another lakefront site, which instantly earns our approval: even the exposed wood latrine seems scenic. A couple of days is all one needs to acclimatize to nature, where everything takes longer, tastes better, and feels more alive. No wonder Thomson and the Group of Seven called Algonquin their spiritual home.

Returning to the access point, we decompress in Voyageur Quest's rustic yet comfortable island cabin, enjoying solar-powered comfort, warm beds, a rejuvenating floating sauna, and a 360-degree view of Kawawaymog Lake. Suitably calibrated by our canoe trip, the scenery appears more vivid, the sound of lapping water as soothing as lip balm. I can only imagine what all this is like in fall, when the foliage explodes into a riot of colour, attracting visitors from around the world. Mind you, the paintings of Thomson and the Group of Seven do it for me. At the peaceful McMichael Gallery, located in Kleinberg, just forty minutes north of Toronto, I see the now-familiar jack pine, spruce, cedar, and birch trees standing tall among the rock of the Canadian Shield, and reflected in Algonquin's dramatic skies and calming waters. Like the lingering taste of an unforgettable meal, the famous art of Algonquin is already calling us back. Back to the lakes. Back to the wild. Back to the canoe.

START HERE: canadianbucketlist.com/algonquin

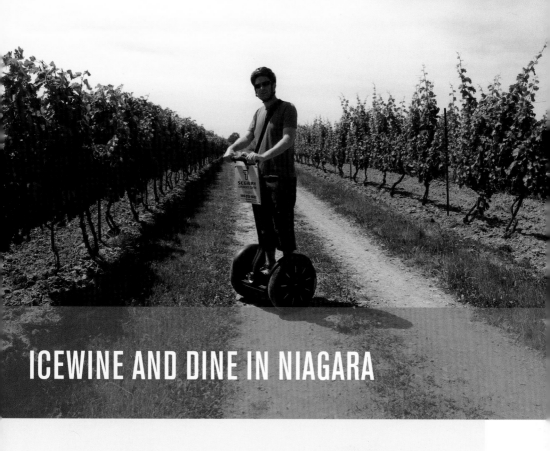

ICEWINE AND DINE IN NIAGARA

Canadians didn't invent icewine, but we sure perfected it. A notable achievement, considering this sweet elixir is one of the riskiest, toughest, and most labour-intensive wines to make. Healthy grapes must be frozen on the vine, hand-picked and pressed within a matter of hours, squeezing out those sweet, valuable, and industry-scrutinized drops.

Niagara is Canada's largest wine region, famed for its Riesling and Chardonnay. As in B.C.'s Okanagan and Nova Scotia's Annapolis Valley, the seductive allure of life among vines has led to a boom in wineries and first-class restaurants. Niagara, blessed with ideal climatic conditions created by Lake Ontario and the Niagara Escarpment, feels like a fat grape bursting with goodness. No wonder other varietals are making their mark: Merlot, Pinot Noir, Baco Noir, Sauvignon Blanc.

ONTARIO

Canada's Best Wine

After a humble start, Canadian wines now compete on the world stage for quality and taste. Angela Aiello, a wine expert, wine writer, and founder of the popular social wine club iYellow-Wine Club, (iyellowwineclub.com) raises a glass to her Top 10 Canadian wines:

1. Flat Rock Cellars Twisted, VQA, Twenty Mile Bench, ON
2. Huff Estates Winery South Bay Chardonnay, VQA, Prince Edward County, ON
3. Mission Hill Reserve Merlot, VQA, Okanagan Valley, BC
4. Henry of Pelham Baco Noir Reserve, VQA, St. Catharines, ON
5. Inniskillin Vidal Icewine, VQA, Niagara-on-the-Lake, ON
6. Closson Chase Chardonnay, VQA, Prince Edward County, ON
7. Benjamin Bridge Nova 7, Gaspereau Valley, NS
8. Le Clos Jordanne Village Reserve Pinot Noir, VQA, Twenty Mile Bench, Niagara, ON
9. Thirty Bench Riesling, VQA, Beamsville Bench, ON
10. Château des Charmes Equuleus, VQA, Niagara-on-the-Lake, ON ➤

Karen's Ice House Slushy Recipe

Icewine is magical to share, and here's a fantastic recipe to spread the love around. Since I discovered it, it's become my go-to at dinner parties.

6 to 10 ice cubes
200 mL Vidal icewine

Blend, adding ice cubes until frothy.
Toasts 8 to 10

My Segway rolls gently along rows of Cabernet Franc as Daniel Speck, one of three brothers behind Henry of Pelham Estate, explains the magic. Warm wind rolls off the lake and gets trapped by the escarpment, circulating to allow grapes to reach their full potential. Among some of the healthiest vines I've ever seen, he points out the wind machines that have revolutionized wine in the region. Essentially stationary helicopter turbines, the blades suck in warm air from higher altitudes, rotating it across the vines in emergencies to prevent devastating frost. It all helps with the consistency needed to produce quality product, and to further Canada's claim as a major winemaking country.

Segway tours, offered at the estate, scoot between vines as I learn about Henry of Pelham's long history and the brothers' devotion to their craft. It makes the icewine tasting back in the dark, cool cellars all the more enjoyable. Niagara introduced the world to a Cabernet Franc icewine — light ruby-red heaven. The first drops on my tongue explode with notes of sweet strawberry jam. The Riesling is more complex, departing with a citrus aftertaste. Vidal, a sturdy grape that is the most popular icewine variety in Niagara, is a pounder, a deliriously delicious full-frontal assault of velvet.

"We need to think of icewine as a condiment, a side dish," explains Daniel. "It should be enjoyed at the start of the meal, paired with spicy and salty dishes, or just enjoyed as dessert on its own." Drinking icewine after a rich, sweet dessert can throw your appetite a life vest made of concrete. Icewine before lunch, on the other hand, is rather decadent, so I head off to Beamsville's Good Earth Restaurant and Cooking School, driving past rows of grapes basking in the sun. My wine philosophy is simple: the bottle is never as important as whom you're sharing it with — in this case, Good Earth's firecracker owner-operator, Nicolette Novak.

Having grown up on the farm before chasing adventure in the city, she moved back to open the region's first cooking school, creating an intimate space in which to pair her favourite things: food and wine. Today the restaurant attracts both locals and visitors, who are drawn by her exceptional dishes, such as house-smoked salmon with homegrown asparagus on flatbread and a lobster and shrimp burger. There's also the orange-hued romantic ambience to be enjoyed under the summer umbrellas; the terrific service; aromas wafting from the open-plan outdoor kitchen; and great musical performances by local artists. Good Earth's wit, candour, and laughs dispense with wine's traditional haughtiness — a reminder of the importance of soul on any plate and in any glass.

After stopping off at Inniskillin, Canada's most famous icewine producer and its earliest pioneer, I pull into a small operation called Ice House, run by one of the world's most experienced icewine makers, Jamie Macfarlane. *Life is too short for cheap wine* reads a sign hanging at the door, a reminder that the cost and difficulty of making icewine justify its expense. I'm greeted by Jamie's wife, Karen, beaming with pride at her products. She pairs my tastings with wasabi peas, lime-chili chips from Australia, and dark chocolate. The rich flavour of Macfarlane's icewine explodes on my tongue, revealing complex flavours: a dazzling meal for my senses. "Icewine is the sweetest kiss," muses Karen, who sealed her own wedding to Jamie with a mouthful of icewine. "It asks you: are you special enough to enjoy this?"

I leave Ice House refreshing myself with an icewine slushy, the perfect accompaniment to a hot summer day, and wonder how far I can take it. At Peller Estates, one of Niagara's largest wineries, you can take it very, very far indeed. In the award-winning, family-run

estate's restaurant, I start with an icewine cosmopolitan. The meal begins: foie gras, tuna tartare spiced with Cabernet Franc icewine, Green bean salad with truffles, paired with Ice Cuvée Classic, Peller's sparkling wine, topped with icewine for sweetness. Icewine-poached lobster-stuffed ravioli, heritage beef served with quinoa and dried berries (rehydrated with icewine, of course). Each course is paired with an excellent Peller wine, building up to the finale: a glass of Signature Series Vidal Icewine. I hold the smooth liquid on my tongue, letting its acidity bloom.

Icewine's freezing origins somehow warm the soul. For its distinctly Canadian flavour — encompassing its food, wine, and people — visiting Niagara's wine region is easily one for the bucket list.

START HERE: canadianbucketlist.com/niagara

ONTARIO

HIKE THE BRUCE TRAIL

Realistically, few people are going to complete the entire 885-kilometre Bruce Trail in one shot. Who has the time or stamina to spend a full month hiking thirty kilometres a day?

Snaking along the Niagara Escarpment, through Bruce County, Canada's oldest and longest walking trail is a challenge best experienced in stages, a goal for a lifetime. The escarpment's limestone cliffs, waterfalls, and creeks offer plenty of eye candy. Day hikers might start with the Walter's Fall Loop or stroll to the Devil's Monument in Dyer's Bay. Other highlights include the two-and-a-half-kilometre Rockway Falls trail southwest of St. Catharines and hiking to the old stone furnace found on the Forks of the Credit near Belfountain.

START HERE: canadianbucketlist.com/hike-bruce-trail

LEARN FROM THE ROCKS

People inhabited the so-called New World for thousands of years before Europeans arrived, their legacy told in the culture, language, and myths of today's First Nations. This makes Petroglyphs Provincial Park, site of the largest concentration of aboriginal rock art in Canada, all the more important. Nine hundred symbolic carvings of humans, objects, and animals were carved between 600 and 1,100 years ago into a single slab of marble. Cherished and utilized like an ancient photo gallery, elders would remove protective moss and use the rocks to introduce new generations to the story of the Ojibwa people. The Teaching Rocks, as they are known, remain a hallowed and sacred site to this day.

The park, a National Historic Site, is a fifty-five-kilometre drive from Peterborough. From there, it's a short walk from the visitor centre to the humidity-controlled glass building that protects the petroglyphs. Visitors often feel a peaceful energy and sense of calm inside the park, especially when hiking the surrounding trails. There are information boards and staff are available to answer questions, and you can also have a seat and watch a twenty-minute video in the visitor centre in which some of the legends are revealed.

Ontario's Teaching Rocks are a very physical reminder that Canada's cultural history stretches back farther, and is far richer, than it is often given credit for.

START HERE: canadianbucketlist.com/petroglyph

ONTARIO ↑

SKATE THE RIDEAU

I'm having coffee with some local friends in Ottawa, and one of the guys at the table starts talking about the Rideau Canal. He's not harping on the fact that it is the "best-preserved slack-water canal in North America, demonstrating the use of European technology on a large scale." We both don't know exactly what that means, but that's the quote from UNESCO's website recognizing the canal as a World Heritage Site. It's way cooler to think of this 202-kilometre-long waterway as the very reason Canada is not part of the United

States, since this military-built engineering achievement allowed the British to defend the country against attacking Americans. Some historians believe that if the canal didn't exist, neither might Canada.

Cooler still is the fact that every winter the Rideau turns into the world's largest outdoor skating rink. At 7.8 kilometres, the skateable section that cuts through Ottawa is equivalent to ninety Olympic-sized hockey rinks. The Rideau used to be the world's longest skateable rink, until Winnipeg took the title with its 8.54-kilometre-long Assiniboine River Trail. Now there's an upstart in Invermere, British Columbia, hoping to usurp both with its Whiteways Trail system on Lake Windermere. Ottawa's wide, Winnipeg's long. When it comes to the ego of a city, size does matter.

Back to the coffee table in Ottawa. It's a frosty -12°C outside, and the beans taste particularly good. "You know, the Rideau, it's a magical place," says my friend. "Sometimes, at midnight, I put on my speedskates, crank some music on my iPod, and I just go for it. I mean, I just skate fast and smooth, and it feels like I'm flying. Nothing beats that feeling — nothing."

He tells it the way he feels it, with deep respect and awe. His experience axel-jumps over the historical significance of the Rideau. It spirals around the quirky fact that Ottawans skate to work, briefcases in hand. It makes my hair stand up and my heart quicken. I want to know that feeling.

That evening, I walk to Kilometre Zero, not far from the steps of Parliament. I only have one night to chase the experience, but there are some challenges to overcome. The fragrance of fresh-fried Beaver Tails wafts in the air, demanding a detour. Exquisite ice sculptures on display from the annual Winterlude Festival prove an additional distraction. I don't even have skates, but to the rescue are rental booths on the skateway. Everything is set, when the final two hurdles present themselves:

1. I ice-skate with the grace of a duck on skis.
2. The ice is in no condition to be skated on.

Ottawa has enjoyed an unseasonably warm winter, and the result is a skateway cracked and scarred, pockmarked and as uneven as a politician's ethics. The locals know when to steer clear, but poor tourists are discovering that ice is very hard, and that an outdoor canal differs greatly from a smooth indoor skating rink. An ambulance flashes and some helpful volunteers cart off a skater. On the way, they tell me I'm mad even to think about being on the ice. The fact that I can barely stand up on ice skates (cut the immigrant a break!) isn't helping.

I close my eyes, take a deep breath, and imagine myself skating at speed, under the bright stars, perhaps an artist like Ottawa's Kathleen Edwards dreamily cooing away on my headphones. Then I slip, land hard on my butt, and quickly decide the only sane place for a tourist in Ottawa right now is a warm pub in the ByWard Market district. Which is exactly where I go.

So I never did quite get to skate the Rideau in all its glory. But that shouldn't stop us from adding it to the Great Central Canada Bucket List.

START HERE: canadianbucketlist.com/rideau

LEAN OFF THE CN TOWER

O ver the years, I've built a reputation as something of a thrill-seeker. Trust me, I never set out to run with bulls, jump out of planes, swing from bridges and dive with sharks. Yet one thing led to another, and a former desk-jobber morphed into the travel guy with a regular magazine column called Thrillseeker. So you're probably thinking: "Of course Esrock would choose to walk outside on one of the world's tallest free-standing structures. It's probably something he does every day." Not quite, but I have walked around the edge of Macau's 233-metre Skytower, shortly before I bungee jumped off the damn thing.

The EdgeWalk is over 100 metres higher than that, and the view over Lake Ontario and the city beats anything Macau, much less anywhere else, has to offer. Sucked in by the CN Tower's vortex, I

decided to join a group of tourists ranging in age from twenty-three to sixty-eight. Piercing the sky, head and shoulders above anything else, Canada's most iconic building landmark was declared a Wonder of the Modern World by the American Society of Civil Engineers. It is a true engineering marvel, 553.33 metres at almost pure vertical, beautifully illuminated at night to become more than just an observation deck and communications tower. The CN Tower is construction as art, Canadian ingenuity at scale, a soaring symbol of Toronto and beyond. Why wouldn't you want to step outside on its rim, put your toes over the edge and place the world at your feet?

Danger? Come on, people, this is one of Canada's busiest tourist attractions. Even though we sign the customary waiver, the emphasis on safety is miles ahead of similar attractions I've encountered in Asia and New Zealand. After all, this is the world's highest full-circle, hands-free walk, and we will be walking on a 1.5-metre ledge 356 metres aboveground on the Tower's main pod.

After taking a Breathalyzer test for alcohol and drugs, we are asked to lock up all loose items — watches, earrings, wallets, necklaces — and slip on a red-rocket walksuit. Our harnesses are checked and quadruple-checked, shoes tightened (twice), glasses attached with string, hair tied up. I see familiar looks of: I don't know why I'm doing this, but I must do it all the same.

You can see every one of the CN Tower's 116 storeys in the elevator as you ascend the external glass-faced shaft. Suddenly the height becomes real. Suddenly the only illustrious CN Tower record I can remember is that 360, the restaurant located 351 metres up, holds the Guinness World Record for the World's Highest Wine Cellar.

In a small control centre, alongside a monitor recording wind speeds and weather, we get clipped in (twice, with additional zip ties) to a steel overhead track. You've more chance of spontaneously combusting than of slipping out of this contraption. Our affable guide, Christian, tells me that although he's undergone extensive training, his only qualification for the job was his healthy fear of heights. Empathy with clients is a natural asset.

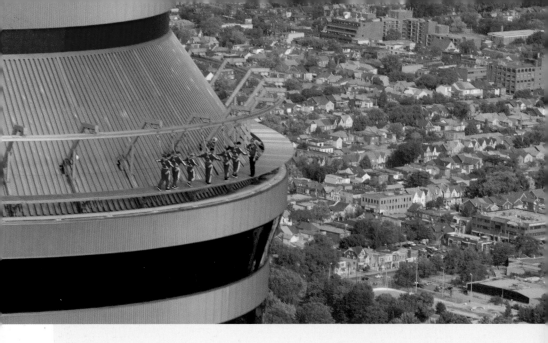

He leads us onto the metal walkway and invites us to walk right up to the edge, our toes hanging over. Even though I know we're safer up here than the folks in the Hot Wheels–sized cars stuck in traffic below, my mind does its best to convince me that leaning over the edge of the CN Tower is not something my body should do. Fortunately, I stopped listening to myself years ago, so I follow my fellow EdgeWalkers pushing their limits and shuffle up to the edge. We applaud our efforts, swap high-fives and breathe in the sweeping view below.

As the walk continues around the Tower, we hit the windy side, with 53-kilometre-an-hour gusts of warm air instantly pickling our adrenal glands. Christian has to holler to point out landmarks. This time he encourages us to lean forward over the edge, on our tiptoes. Each challenge is ably met, so by the time the group returns to the sheltered side, facing the sea that is Lake Ontario on a day so clear I can make out the buildings at Niagara Falls, everyone is comfortable enough to lean back and smile for the photos. Arms outstretched, heels balanced on the edge, we embrace the sky with huge smiles on our faces. You don't have to be a thrill-seeker to benefit from a little edge.

START HERE: canadianbucketlist.com/edgewalk

MOTORBIKE AROUND SUPERIOR

Lake Superior doesn't give up her dead. The water of the world's largest lake by area is so cold, bodies sink to its depths. Mortality was on my mind as I nervously tucked into pancakes in the crowded Hoito Finnish Diner in Thunder Bay.

You have to admit, a writer getting killed in a motorcycle accident while researching a book about things to do before you die has just the sort of ironic twist you'd find in a newspaper story. Granted, I'd already walked face-first off a cliff, scuba dived wrecks, and driven many a long moose-trapped highway, but the challenge ahead was particularly and personally daunting. My wife and my mother were in full fret mode over my plan to research one of the great motorcycle trips of Canada: the north shore of Lake Superior. So what if I'd never been on a bike trip before? So what if my saddle hours, including my licence training, could be counted on two fingers? So what if the most powerful bike I'd ever ridden was 125 cc? And so what if a car did T-bone my scooter,

breaking my knee and cracking my helmet? That accident kick-started my grand adventure, my rebirth as an adventurer!

I've faced so many limit-pushing challenges in the many years since then that I've learned the secret to getting through just about anything. Douglas Adams boldly put it in his futuristic travel book *The Hitchhiker's Guide to the Galaxy*. When Larry Lage, owner of Thunder Bay's Excalibur Motorcycle Works, hands me a jacket and gloves, he doesn't notice that under my thin-lipped smile I'm muttering my most powerful mantra:

Don't Panic.

Riding a motorcycle on the shores of mighty Lake Superior, as I was quick to discover, is one part exhilaration, one part speed, a dash of freedom, a lime wedge of danger, topped off with camaraderie and natural beauty to make a cocktail of mobile magic. No wonder this 700-kilometre stretch of the Trans-Canada from Thunder Bay to

Sault Ste. Marie has such an amazing reputation with bikers. Wavy S-curves on smooth blacktop cutting through forest and rock, always close to sparkling blue lake, the north shore attracts riders from across the continent, some of whom complete the 2,100-kilometre loop around Superior on scenic roads in the United States.

Larry had loaned me his Kawasaki KWR 650 dual-sport bike, its odometer a third of the way through its second (or third) rotation. The bike is reliable and experienced, much like my biking buddy Steve Kristjanson. A semi-retired jack-of-all-trades, Steve has seen thousands of kilometres in the saddle, having ridden to the Soo and back in one stretch: a 1,400-kilometre sitting. Our goal is half that in double the time, two days on the road, stopping at viewpoints and attractions along the way.

We start by paying homage to Terry Fox at his memorial just outside Thunder Bay. Here was a boy who was running across Canada, racked with cancer, on one leg. His legacy — hundreds of millions of dollars raised for cancer research — is an inspiration and further steel to arm my own courage for the incomparably lighter challenge ahead.

Still, it doesn't stop me from stalling my bike at a highway intersection, right next to Larry and his bike-instructor girlfriend Diane, who are accompanying us to the Ouimet Canyon. I expect Larry to point me right back to his shop, but he gamely encourages me instead. "Keep your head up, and look where you want to go, not at whatever you're going to hit," adds Diane, like a supportive parent. These guys live and breathe their bikes, a world apart from the

One Week

In the 2008 film *One Week*, Joshua Jackson plays a mild Torontonian named Ben who discovers he has terminal cancer. He promptly buys a 1973 Norton Commando motorcycle and decides to ride to Vancouver Island, a road trip so intrinsically Canadian even the Tragically Hip's Gord Downie shows up in a cameo. On his journey, Ben encounters the world's biggest nickel in Sudbury, ponders Terry Fox outside Thunder Bay and takes snaps of the world's biggest camel, tipi, hockey stick, and muskie. Ben would have liked this book. ➤

annoying twits on decibel-shattering cruisers, content to just parade them. I'm told the biggest dangers are moose and deer, which can run out of the ditches straight into your path. Warning signs line the highway, and I spot the occasional cross in the ground commemorating one who didn't heed them. Steve hit a deer a couple of years ago going sixty, broke his knee and killed the animal. He knows he got off lightly.

Visor down, I smooth into the groove of the road. The slightest movement of my hand on the throttle has an instant effect, slowing me

A Wild Goose Chase

Among the roadside attractions you'll encounter, look out for Wawa's famous Canada goose. It's the largest statue of its kind and claims to be one of Canada's most photographed landmarks. Dating back to the early 1960s, the 8.5-metre steel bird was built to encourage passing traffic on the Trans-Canada Highway to come into Wawa. Today, Wawa's goose even has its own webcam. ➤

down, hurling me forward. We pass through the glowing ridge at Red Rocks, stopping to admire magnificent views of this sea-lake. With a surface area of 82,100 square kilometres, Lake Superior contains a whopping 10 percent of all the surface freshwater on the planet. It creates its own weather system, supports fisheries and tourism, and each winter generates waves up to 2.5 metres high, to the delight of some truly hard-core and well-insulated surfers.

After dinner in Rossport, we check out the Aguasabon River Gorge before stopping for the night in the small mill town of Terrace Bay. We ride in on a newly tarred stretch of highway candy, as smooth and black as licorice. Steve lubes the chains, checks the tires and oil, a picture of Zen with his art of motorcycle maintenance. It's a relief to get out of my sweat-soaked biker gear, a relief that my only crash today is in the soft bed of the Imperial Motel.

Thick fog blows in ominously the following morning. Moose had crashed into my anxious dreams. Come on, Esrock, get a grip! Yes, motorcycles are more likely to lead to accidents, and having felt the wind slam against my chest at a hundred kilometres an hour, I know there's little room for error. Yet the highway is wide and forgiving, traffic relatively light, overtaking lanes frequent.

We ride into the spooky fog in staggered formation, brights on, speed down. Droplets of moisture cling to my visor, so I use my gloved hand to wipe it clean. The roar of the engine, the blur of green forest, the steam rising off lakes in the shadows: even in the fog, the adventure is . . . superior! Gradually, visibility improves, the clouds providing some welcome shelter from the unusually hot sun. I take a photo in White River, where Winnie, the bear that inspired the children's books, was born. When we reach the landmark Wawa Goose overlooking the valley, I'm still wondering what a Pooh is. The sandy beach and overlooking cliffs at Old Women's Bay are gorgeous, as is the view of the lake islands from Alona Bay.

I'm getting comfortable on the bike, accustomed to the speed, the wind, the vibration beneath me. Next time you find yourself behind a bike on the highway, watch what happens when it passes another bike going in the opposite direction. The left hand points out, wrist slightly twisted, for the friendly biker "wave." Everybody does it, like the secret handshake of some exclusive club. Everyone except three riders on Harleys, whom Steve, riding a rare Suzuki DR800, dismisses as posers anyway.

By the time we reach Batchawana Bay, stopping to enjoy a cold reward beer at Voyageurs, I feel as if I've overcome my own poser problems. Other than three deer crossing the road, the risk was benign. Whatever ghosts were haunting my nerves had been winterized in the garage. Lake Superior, with waters that never give up her dead, energized me with a rush of life.

Bike stored outside the hotel in Sault Ste. Marie, I text a biker friend back home to let him know I made it safely. He replies in seconds. "Makes you appreciate your life knowing you can die at any moment hey?"

No, it makes you appreciate life knowing you can conquer your fears.

START HERE: canadianbucketlist.com/superior

Fall Foliage on the Bucket List

Every September in central Canada, the temperature drops and the days get noticeably shorter. Maple, birch, poplar, and red oak leaves expel oxygen, beginning a process that will see them wither and, as the season suggests, fall to the ground. A welcome by-product of this cycle is the incredible array of colours that result from the leaves' death throes. Rich maroons, cabernet reds, bright egg-yolk yellows, and glowing oranges explode in such spectacular fashion that visitors travel from all over the world just to experience them in all their glory. The following are some of the best places to view the fall foliage in Central Canada:

Agawa Canyon Train Tour: Sault Ste. Marie, ON

Operated by Algoma Central Railway, this scenic passenger train departs daily from Sault Ste. Marie, and travels 183 kilometres north through forest, lake country, and along the granite cliffs of the Canadian Shield. The locomotive features large viewing windows, GPS-triggered tour narration available in five languages, and excellent dining. Once you arrive at Canyon Park (accessible only by train or hiking), you have ninety minutes to explore five easy walking trails, including a seventy-six-metre-high canyon lookout. Fall foliage tends to be best during the last two weeks of September and in the first week of October. Like they did with Algonquin Park (another fall foliage hotspot), the Group of Seven artists captured Agawa Canyon's beauty with a number of famous landscape paintings.

Lanaudiére and Mauricie, QC

Located between Montreal and Quebec City, this regional fall foliage favourite is home to ten thousand lakes and hundreds of forests and parks. There are also a number of attractive small towns and villages to explore in the area. To see the colours, head into the 536-square-kilometre woodland of La Mauricie National Park, where you can drive, hike, walk, or canoe in amongst the foliage. The region also offers various road trip itineraries that trace the heritage of New France, crossing back and forth over Canada's first overland route, the Chemin du Roy.

Peterborough, ON

Two and a half hours from Ottawa and ninety minutes from Toronto, Peterborough and the Kawarthas are a popular weekend autumn escape. Here you'll find plenty of cabin and B&B getaways, over a hundred lakes, and the largest wilderness preserve south of the Algonquin Park. After freaking out at the foliage, adventurous bucket listers should check out the Warsaw Caves and Conservation area. Having explored the subterranean activity park, you'll emerge from the dark depths to sparkling reds, oranges, and yellows. Since 1868, the region's Norwood Fall Fair has been a Thanksgiving tradition, and is located just a short drive east of Peterborough.

The Laurentians, QC

It might be getting a little chilly in Mont Tremblant to bike Le P'tit Train du Nord (see page 70), but that shouldn't stop you from heading to the Laurentian Mountains in the fall. This 22,000-square-kilometre region north of Montreal offers up some of the best fall foliage in the country. The mountain air is crisp, the maple groves are glowing, and romance blossoms in the villages, spas, and resorts. Besides the attraction of the autumn foliage, it's a great time to sample the seasonal gourmet food produced in the area, including fabulous cheeses, wines, ciders, sausages, honey, and maple syrup products. ➤

EXPLORE THE GREAT MUSEUMS

The word *museum* sounds awfully like *mausoleum* — a place where artifacts go to die. Fortunately, Canada's great museums are anything but, having been revitalized into living temples of knowledge where one can interact with, discover, and journey to far-off places, without ever leaving the building.

Let's begin our brief guided tour in Ottawa, home to a half-dozen national museums, where locals and visitors learn all about Canada and beyond. We start in the National Gallery, housing the country's largest collection of Canadian art. The brainchild of renowned Canadian architect Moshe Safdie, the Great Hall is entered into via a long ramp, designed to put visitors in the right frame of mind to experience the art to come. The Great Hall uses windows and skylights to create an exceptionally light space, cleverly avoiding direct contact with the art itself while offering famous views

ONTARIO

of the Parliament Buildings. Safdie was inspired by the Library of Parliament, so much so that the Great Hall has a volume identical to that of Parliament's stone library, which lies across the Ottawa River. Besides iconic works from Canadian greats from throughout history, the museum also features works by Rembrandt, Van Gogh, Matisse, Monet, Picasso, Warhol, and Pollock. You can't miss the gallery's distinctive glass entrance, or Louise Bourgeois's creepy spider outside.

We then walk across the Ottawa River along the Alexandra Bridge and into Gatineau, Quebec. It takes just twenty minutes to reach the beautifully designed Canadian Museum of History, the most-visited museum in the country. Over the next few years, the former Canadian Museum of Civilization will be renovating half of its permanent space, introducing new galleries to complement old favourites. We enter through the Grand Hall, with its view of the river and Parliament Hill, under towering totem poles (the largest

display in the world), to Haida artist Bill Reid's original plaster of his masterpiece *Spirit of Haida Gwaii*. It's a fitting introduction to the first level, the First People's Hall, tracing twenty thousand years of Aboriginal history in Canada. With the renovation, the former Canada Hall, Canadian Personalities Hall, and Canadian Postal Museum have been combined to create the largest exhibition of Canadian history ever assembled. Unaffected by the refurbishment is the Canadian Children's Museum, where kids will continue to embed themselves in new worlds, literally getting passports as they learn how people live around the world.

Ottawa's other national museums are well worth investigating: the Museum of Nature, the Canadian Agriculture Museum, the Canadian Aviation and Space Museum, the Canadian Science and Technology Museum, and the haunting Canadian War Museum, with its jarring structural angles and captivating human stories.

ONTARIO

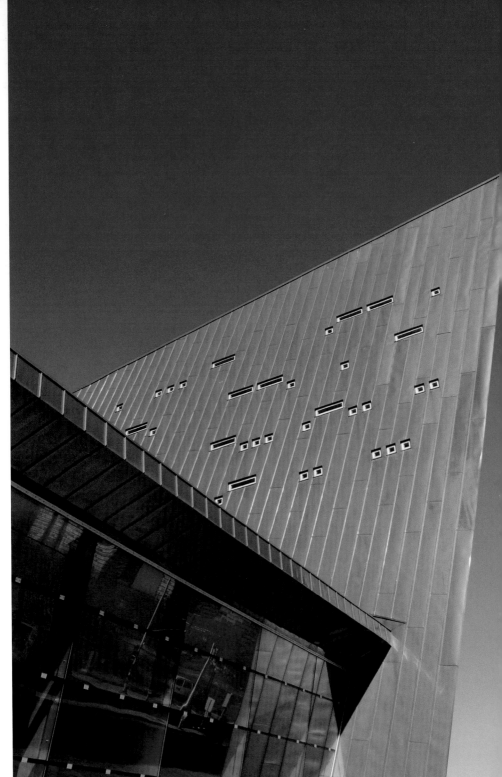

Still in Ontario, let's Porter (verb: to fly affordably) to Toronto and take a gander at T-Dot's prized museums. The Royal Ontario Museum, or ROM, is the largest cultural and natural history museum in Canada, and the most popular and most visited museum in the city. Star architect Daniel Libeskind's futuristic Crystal looks as if a Transformer crashed into a heritage building — which works to attract more than one million visitors annually to the museum's forty galleries. With over six million items, the ROM has something for everybody, and plenty left over. I love the Dinosaur Gallery, the giant totem pole, and the creepy Gallery of Birds, forever flying nowhere.

Not far away, on Dundas Street, is the Art Gallery of Ontario, one of the largest gallery spaces in North America, with a collection of over eighty thousand works from the first century to the present. Residing in its Georgian manor premises since 1910, the AGO continues to host some of the world's most important art exhibitions, introducing visitors to the Old Masters, King Tut and the Pharoahs, along with priceless works from the Hermitage and India's Royal Courts.

Yes, Canada's great museums are very much alive, treasured by anyone interested in culture, history, art, and science. Prized and appreciated, therefore, by anyone ticking off the Central Canada Bucket List.

START HERE: canadianbucketlist.com/museums

On the Bucket List With: Kevin Callan

Broadcaster and author of the bestselling series The Happy Camper, *Kevin Callan (kevincallan.com) is one of Canada's best-known canoeists and outdoorsmen.*

Hidden amongst the rugged Penokean Hills, north of Elliot Lake, is a cluster of aqua-blue lakes and crystal-clear streams, all alive with trophy self-sustaining rainbow — a rarity that only occurs in one percent of Canada's waterways. This is one of northern Ontario's absolute gems. After you explore it for the first time, you'll be returning — guaranteed.

Blue Fox Camp acts as the best base to tour the area. The lodge is the centrepiece of the region and is located on the bottom end of Kirkpatrick Lake (known locally as Blue Lake). From here, countless lakes, ponds, streams, as well as the White River, provide dreamlike settings to unpack a fishing rod and drop a fly. The best access is [via] a bush plane. Some logging roads exist to the north, but they don't give you full reach to the best places to fish. Beside, it's the difficulty of access that's kept this place so special. Timber Wolf Air in Blind River is your best choice.

It's an incredible story: a logging camp, changed over to a fishing camp, now in the midst of changing over to a futuristic conservation retreat for fish-lovers who like to catch-and-release trophy rainbow trout stocked over seventy years ago. It doesn't get any better then this.

Kevin Callan ➤

ONTARIO

SUPPORT THE BLUE JAYS

I'm entering the big leagues, ready to play hardball and cover my bases so I can knock this one out of the park. Although it might come out of left field, I'm going to say this right off the bat: I've never been to a baseball game, never so much as watched a baseball game on TV, and other than reading the book *Moneyball*, I can't tell the singles from the shutouts. "Say it ain't so, Joe!" but it's the truth. I grew up watching cricket, which bowls out North Americans the way baseball throws a curveball at cricket fans. Still, I can appreciate that the Toronto Blue Jays are no grandstanding bush-league team. They're the only Canadian team in the major leagues, the only other part of the World that currently qualifies for the World Series, and as such, supporting them at home deserves a spot on our bucket list.

My first impression, as I enjoy the view inside the stadium from the Renaissance Hotel's Arriba Restaurant, is that these guys can throw. How their arms stay in their sockets is a mystery, as the Blue Jays warm up for their opening match in a series against the Los Angeles Angels. The retractable roof of the Rogers Centre is open to allow the ballpark to bask in the glorious late June sun. Satiated with beer from Arriba (at considerably less than what you might pay for it in the stadium), I hop over to the stadium and take my seat in the modest crowd a dozen rows up to the left of home plate. It's been decades since the Blue Jays' glory days of 1992–93, when they won back-to-back World Series — Canada's first World Series titles. Since then, up to the time of writing, they hadn't made the playoffs.

Poor Toronto sports fans, forever supporting their underdog hockey, basketball, and baseball teams.

Still, this is the big league, and the atmosphere is festive, especially with the year's star player, Jose Bautista, smashing home runs out of the park. When he steps up to bat, the stadium simmers with anticipation, and the pitcher throws more balls than usual. I explain to my wife, poorly, that a ball is a pitch that does not qualify for a strike. She tells me I should just stick to cricket, since the only balls she can see are those being thrown, and possibly the ones on the fielder with the too-tight pants.

We watch as a pitch is fouled off into the crowd, causing a mosh pit frenzy to claim the ball. Not only is it perfectly possible for a whizzing baseball to bean an inattentive fan, but it's expected that surrounding fans will trample them to hell in hopes of leaving with a souvenir. In cricket, I might add, the ball is tossed back into the field of play.

Somewhere in the middle of the game, Bautista hits a huge home run with the bases loaded, and I'm on my feet with the rest of them, cheering the four players running around the diamond. That's the moment I was looking for, right there, an instant of support and momentary triumph with the CN Tower looming overhead. We follow the game as best we can, understanding that it appears to be coming right down to the bottom of the ninth, in which the bases are loaded and a Blue Jays home run would sneak a victory right out from under the mitts of the Angels. Strike one. Strike two. Then, before I can fully build up my excitement, the batter hits the ball directly to an outfielder, the Blue Jays hang their heads and slump their shoulders, the Angels jump up and down, and fans begin to stream out of their seats. As the Blue Jays' newest fans, we look around and notice nobody's too hung up about it. It's the Blue Jays. They're used to this sort of thing. But it won't stop the fans from coming back — not one iota. And it won't stop those of us ticking off bucket lists either.

START HERE: canadianbucketlist.com/bluejays

FEEL THE SPIRIT OF MANITOULIN ISLAND

On the world's largest freshwater lake island, they take the Great Spirit very seriously. For the people of the Ojibwa, Odawa, and Pottawatomi Nations, Manitoulin Island is a land so beautiful that the Great Spirit, the Father of Life, kept it for himself. Today, they welcome guests with a number of authentic aboriginal experiences, providing an opportunity to learn about this unique island directly from its people.

The Great Spirit Circle Trail is a multi-faceted excursion that encompasses the seven First Nation communities on the island. You can pick local teas, medicinal herbs, fruits, and plants, make bannock over open fires, or hike up a dramatic bluff with incredible views of the island and participate in a traditional tobacco ceremony. Walking tours visit heritage museums and galleries, there are storytelling and craft workshops, singing and drumming circles, and overnight stays in traditional teepees. Many guests combine an interest in aboriginal history and culture with the outdoors, taking guided hikes, bicycle rides, or canoe trips on the lake, or horseback riding in the woods. There is nowhere else in the country quite like Manitoulin, a 2,766-square-kilometre island of fascinating culture, stunning natural beauty, and enormous spirit.

START HERE: canadianbucketlist.com/manitoulin

ONTARIO

GIVE A STANDING OVATION AT STRATFORD

"We all hope that in your lives you have just the right amount of sitting quietly at home, and just the right amount of adventure."
—Barnaby Tucker in Thornton Wilder's *The Matchmaker*

When a small town falls on hard times, it needs to reinvent itself. Once a railway junction and manufacturing centre for locomotives, Stratford found itself in an economic pickle until a local journalist named Tom Patterson realized that a town named after Stratford-upon-Avon, sitting on its own Avon River, with a neighbouring town called Shakespeare, should have its own Shakespeare Festival. In the summer of 1953, Alec Guinness uttered the first lines of the first play (in a tent, no less), and the Stratford Shakespeare Festival was born.

10 Famous Actors Who Have Performed at the Festival

1. Christopher Walken (1968)
2. Peter Ustinov (1979–80)
3. Christopher Plummer (1956–2012)
4. Alec Guinness (1953)
5. William Shatner (1954–56)
6. Maggie Smith (1976–80)
7. James Mason (1954)
8. Brian Dennehy (2008, 2011)
9. Jessica Tandy (1976, 1980)
10. John Neville (1983–89)

By the time I visit, sixty years later, Stratford has grown to host one of the largest and most renowned theatre festivals in the world. During its lengthy April-to-November engagement, it attracts some of the world's best actors, directors, designers, and theatre talent. The tent has been replaced by four major theatres, pioneering the thrust stage that allows the audience to surround the actors on three sides, as they would have in Shakespeare's day. Enthusiastic audiences arrive from around the world, with the theatre boom resulting in significant economic aftershocks.

Stratford also boasts one of the best culinary schools in the country; an impressive selection of restaurants, hotels, and theatre schools; and the third-largest costume warehouse in the world. It's

ONTARIO ↑

a town where kids grow up knowing they can make a living in the arts — as actors, stage designers, lighting technicians, or musicians. A fact acknowledged by its most recent celebrity resident, a kid who used to busk outside the Avon Theatre on Downie Street and goes by the name of Justin Bieber. The week before I arrive, Bieber humbly returned to the same spot on the same stairs, guitar in hand, to play a couple of songs. Today, as I enjoy poutine at the Downie Street Burger across the street, a violinist sends his classical notes soaring into the warm summer breeze. Spotless, small downtown Stratford hums with coffee shops, chocolatiers, boutiques, bistros, and bookstores — the kind of place that leaves a whimsical impression and one envious of the thirty-two thousand people who live in a small town with more culture than most major cities.

Live trumpets at the tent-inspired Festival Theatre signal that it's time for the two p.m. matinee of this year's popular farce, *The Matchmaker*. Non-Shakespearean works were introduced as early as the festival's second year, and today include musicals, comedies, Broadway hits, and classic works of world theatre. Thornton Wilder's

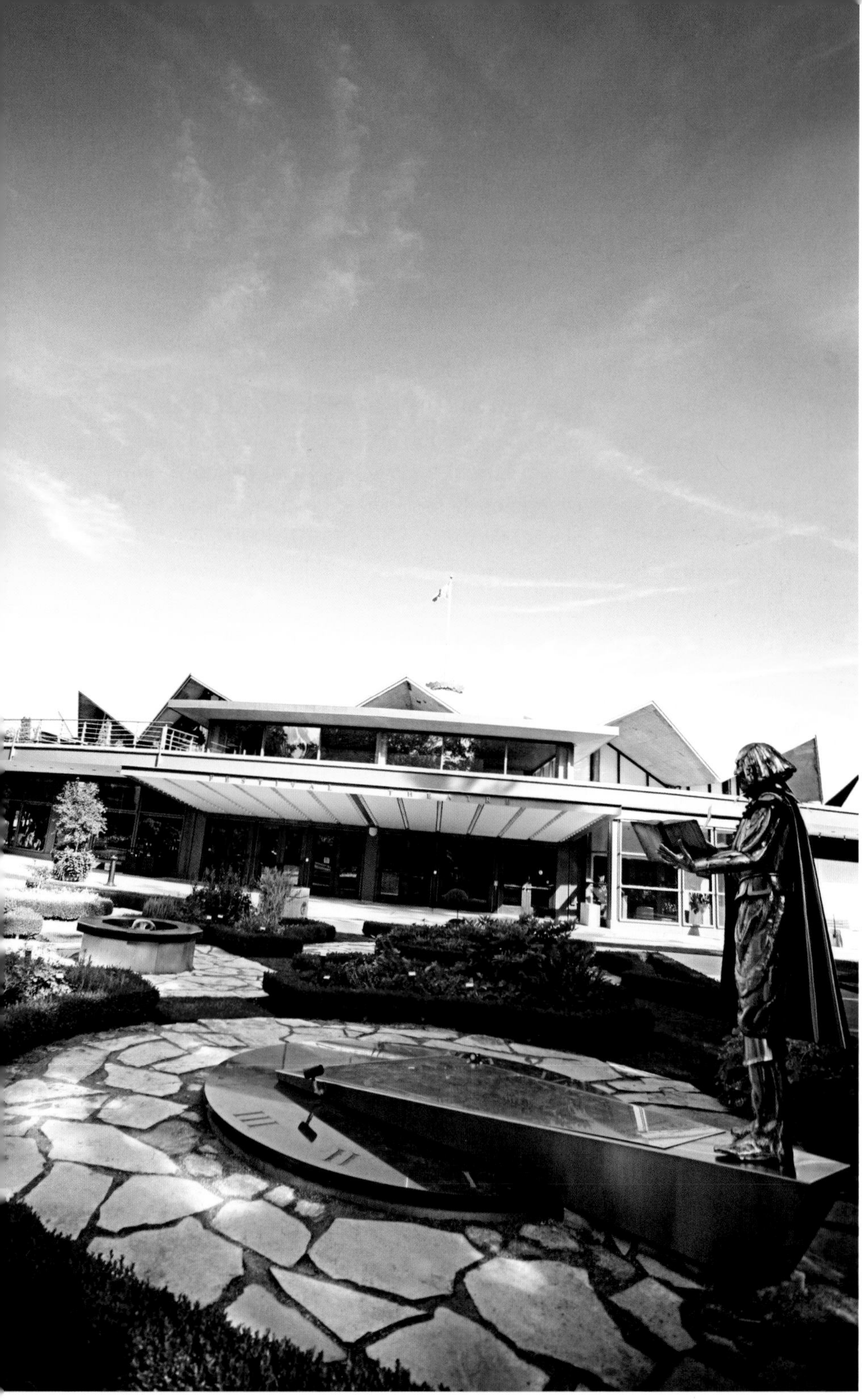

The Matchmaker was the Broadway hit that inspired *Hello, Dolly!* and contains some of the sharpest wit and most crackling situational comedy ever seen onstage. There are several interweaving storylines, but I'm particularly drawn to the tale of two shop clerks, trapped in their work, determined, for one day at least, to have "an adventure." It all leads to love, danger, fear and shenanigans, reflected in blistering one-liners, split-second escapes and an endearing happy ending. The performances are fantastic, the stage design stupendous, and two hours later the cast graciously receives a standing ovation from the crowd. On top of the Stratford Shakespeare Festival's many accomplishments, it's this moment of appreciation that bows its way onto our bucket list.

Later, I tour the fascinating costume and prop warehouse, and walk down to the Avon River. Opposite colourful artists displaying their work in the park, swans glide under the scenic arched bridge to Patterson Island. I wonder if Patterson had any notion of the impact his idea would have on the town, its people, and Canada's cultural legacy. Regardless, we can all appreciate the power of reinvention and the special magic that brews when we wake up and decide to chase our own adventures.

START HERE: canadianbucketlist.com/shakespeare

GET SPRAYED IN NIAGARA FALLS

Visiting the tourist zone in the town of Niagara Falls on Canada Day is a classy dream, and by *classy* I mean *tacky*, and by *dream* I mean *nightmare*. Vegas without the spectacle, the tourist zone is designed for sugar-saturated, overstimulated kids dragging along bludgeoned parents with their bruised wallets. Theme rides, water parks, lineups, burger, ice cream, and hot dog joints — on a scorching July 1, it can all seem a bit much. Then I opened the drapes of the honeymooners' suite on the twenty-first floor of the Sheraton to see what had attracted all this madness in the first place.

Never underestimate the impact of seeing Niagara Falls for the first time. This from a guy who's swum in rock pools atop Victoria Falls, speedboated up the tropical canyons of South America's stunning Iguazu Falls, and showered in the cascades of some of the most beautiful waterfalls on six continents. Once I got past the family holiday madness, the crowds, the crawling traffic, and the fifteen-minute wait for the Sheraton's elevators, I could see Niagara Falls for what it

ONTARIO ↑

is: Canada's most spectacular natural wonder, worthy of its draw as one of the world's great tourist attractions.

Draining Lake Erie into Lake Ontario, the American, Bridal, and Horseshoe falls combine to produce the highest flow rate of any waterfall in the world, a volume of water that famously sends mist mushrooming into the sky. It's even more impressive when you consider that massive hydroelectric projects upriver redirect much of the flow before it reaches the twenty-one- to thirty-metre drop of the

On the Wire

June 15, 2012, saw the first tightrope walk across Niagara Falls in 116 years. A seventh-generation tightrope walker, Nik Wallenda walked 550 metres near the base of Horseshoe Falls, watched by millions on television and huge crowds on both sides of the border. Getting permission for the stunt was no easy task, as Canadian authorities in Niagara were worried the stunt would encourage amateurs. Just a few months earlier, an unidentified man scaled a railing and jumped into Horseshoe Falls, becoming the third person to survive an unprotected fall over the Falls. ➤

American Falls and the fifty-three-metre plummet at the horseshoe-shaped crest that separates Canada from the United States.

Given the hyper-commercialization of the town, I enjoyed simply strolling along the promenade on a warm night, watching spotlights illuminate the water, feeling the refreshing spray as I got closer to the thunderous whirlpool beneath Horseshoe Falls. Before the lake waters disappear over the edge, the Falls seem to challenge each visitor with a thought experiment: if I went over the edge, would I survive? Three people have survived after going over unprotected, including a seven-year-old boy, while others have used barrels and protective devices to increase their chances of emerging unscathed. Over the years some have succeeded, others not. Nik Wallenda's tightrope walk in 2012, the first successful attempt in over a century, becomes even more impressive at the scene of his accomplishment. Illegal as it is to attempt it, people will continue to test the might of North America's mightiest falls, on purpose and by accident.

The iconic experience, the must-do-no-matter-how-long-the-lineup, is a gorge cruise. On the Canadian side, Hornblower Niagara

ONTARIO ↑

Cruises' two state-of-the-art catamarans replaced the iconic *Maid of the Mist* boats in 2014 (the *Maid of the Mist* continues to run from the American side). Passengers can choose to stay dry or get wet, depending on where they position themselves: on the outer decks, prepare for a cold-mist baptism beneath the Horseshoe Falls.

The boats take up to seven hundred passengers at a time, doing a blistering trade on the summer's busiest long weekend. Joining the Canada Day mayhem, I expect to be waiting for hours, but the lineup moves quickly and smoothly. Passengers are given pink plastic ponchos and then herded like cattle through various checkpoints before boarding the boat and squeezing onto the upper and lower decks. Soon we're underway, and as we motor along upriver, squeals from the kids greet the first sheet of spray. By the time we retreat from the choppy rapids several minutes later, everyone's head is soaked. Hornblower offers sunrise cruises, cocktails at sunset, and fireworks cruises, too. From the boat, Niagara Falls really looks and sounds like the wild and raging natural wonder it is. With cash in hand, you can take Niagara Parks' Journey Behind the Falls, or take to the skies with Niagara Helicopter's nine-minute ride, or cross the canyon farther downriver in an old-fashioned air tram, or watch a 4-D movie (the extra D means you'll get sprayed with water in the theatre). That's a lot of waterfall action. I was content to enjoy the exceptional view from my hotel room and watch the nightly fireworks. Could I live without the kitsch attractions and loud, wet kids bouncing around in the elevators? Definitely. Is Niagara Falls something to see before you die? Absolutely.

START HERE: canadianbucketlist.com/falls

WATCH THE LEAFS vs. THE HABS

The Great Central Canada Bucket List does not deal in hypotheticals. It doesn't include items such as Play Hoops with Steve Nash, or Go Over Niagara Falls in a Barrel, as thrilling as they both sound. So while I'd love to list Watch Your Team Win Game Seven of the Stanley Cup Finals, the painful reality is that you might never get the opportunity to do so. Most of us will battle to find a ticket if our team actually gets to Game Seven in the first place. That being said, after an exhausting and bruising season, chances are at least two Canadian teams will make it to the annual playoffs, and you just might find yourself in the stands whooping like a crane when they do so.

I cheer for any Canadian team in the playoffs, which I understand violates several hockey codes. I'm told Montreal Canadiens fans would simply never cheer for the Toronto Maple Leafs, and the Calgary Flames would sooner be extinguished than support the slick Edmonton Oilers. Everyone east of B.C. hates the Canucks, but differences can be put aside for the Winnipeg Jets because their logo is so damn cool. All of that being said, whether you're a hockey supporter or not, our bucket list demands that you experience true hockey fever at least once, and thus I find myself at the Air Canada Centre in Toronto, witnessing the oldest rivalry in Canadian hockey.

Canada's Ultimate Hockey Matchup

Toronto and Montreal have faced each other in fifteen playoff series, the last one being in 1979. The Habs have won 8 to the Leafs' 7. **Score: Canadiens 1**

Forbes places the Toronto Maple Leafs as the NHL's Most Valuable Team. The Montreal Canadiens slot in at Number 3, behind the New York Rangers. **Score: Maple Leafs 1**

All-time leading scorer for the Maple Leafs is Mats Sundin (981 games, 420 goals, 987 points). All-time leading scorer for the Habs is Maurice "The Rocket" Richard (1,111 games, 626 goals, 1,091 points). **Score: Canadiens 1**

Number of Stanley Cups: Maple Leafs 13, Canadiens 24. **Score: Canadiens 1**

Final Score: In a closely contested series, I have to give it to the Winnipeg Jets. ➤

I knew this was more than a game when, earlier, I stood on the subway platform in Toronto's College station. Facing me was a mural of Leafs hockey players, and against my back was a mural of Habs players. After quickly checking why the Canadiens are known as the Habs (it's short for *habitants*, the name given to French settlers in New France), I concluded that anything immortalized in subway station art must be important. Since the 1940s, these two teams have come to represent more than just hockey. Each time the skates hit the ice, a national scar gets scratched. The blue Toronto Maple Leafs are a symbol of Canada's British heritage, the English elite that have brokered the financial power among the tall buildings in Canada's biggest city. The red Habs are passionate warriors of the French-Canadian heritage, where emotions run deep and a distinct culture is celebrated. It's the yin-yang dichotomy of Canada, a cultural clash, a historical mash-up, a tale of the country's two biggest cities.

I've always believed there's a connection between the growth of commercial sport and the relatively peaceful times in which we now live. When two nations can vent their frustrations on a soccer pitch or a hockey rink, what need is there to take up axes and spill unnecessary blood? Points can be proven, boasts can be sung, and losers can walk away knowing there is always a next time. Considering that

many of the players are actually from the United States, Scandinavia, Russia, or other parts of Canada, hockey is mostly a fan's battle anyway.

Now, if you mix red and blue together, you get purple, the right colour for the bruising matchup I expected at the Air Canada Centre. I'm told there's no other game in the NHL where you'll hear so many fans cheering for the opposing team. Indeed, there's no shortage of Habs shirts walking about in hostile territory. If this were an English football game, that might be dangerous, but as it stands, I bump into two brothers wearing opposing team sweaters. "How is this possible?" I ask. They explain that they grew up in Montreal, and one brother relocated to Toronto fifteen years ago, adopting his city's team just as surely as I've adopted Canada's national sport.

The mood is festive, a little tense. I head up to the nosebleed section and meet more Montreal fans, engaged in conversation with Leafs regulars the next row up. Perhaps if this were Game Seven (there go the hypotheticals again), or if the light beer wasn't so expensive, there might be some real danger.

The teams come onto the ice, the fans cheer, and Montreal proceeds to give the long-suffering Leafs a 5–0 drubbing. Months later, the Maple Leafs will have their revenge. It's all good fun until someone gets hurt, which strapping young millionaires on ice skates are very well paid to do on our behalf.

Wherever you are in Canada, cheering at a live hockey game that matters is something to do before you're sent to the Great Big Penalty Box in the Sky.

START HERE: canadianbucketlist.com/nhl

ONTARIO ↑

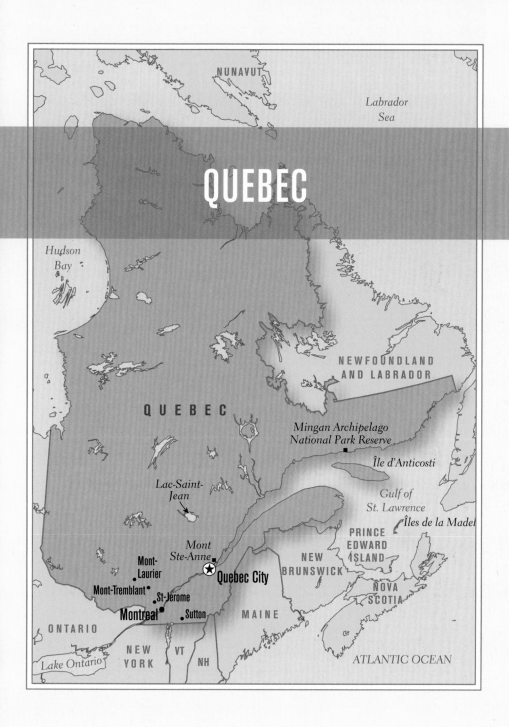

QUEBEC

Labrador
Sea

Hudson
Bay

NUNAVUT

NEWFOUNDLAND
AND LABRADOR

QUEBEC

Mingan Archipelago
National Park Reserve

Île d'Anticosti

Lac-Saint-
Jean

Gulf of
St. Lawrence

Îles de la Madel

Mont
Ste-Anne

Mont-
Laurier

Quebec City

PRINCE
EDWARD
ISLAND

NEW
BRUNSWICK

Mont-Tremblant

St-Jerome

NOVA
SCOTIA

Montreal

Sutton

MAINE

ONTARIO

NEW
YORK

VT

NH

ATLANTIC OCEAN

Lake Ontario

BIKE LE P'TIT TRAIN DU NORD

Picture this: It's Monday morning. You awake in the comfortable bed of a B&B that puts the *charm* in charming. Pack your light bags and head downstairs for breakfast, where the owners, inevitably named Jean-Claude or Bernard or Cedric, greet you with a cup of warm coffee, fresh orange juice, and the choice of a large omelette or French toast served with bananas, raspberries, and custard. Figuring you're going to need the calories, you order the French toast and drown it in rich maple syrup for good measure. You leave your bags at the bottom of the stairs, walk outside, and put water, snacks, cameras, and sunscreen in your bicycle's saddlebags.

Across the street is the crushed-gravel pathway of the longest linear park in Canada, a 230-kilometre bike trail in summer — a ski trail in winter — that runs right through the heart of the Laurentians. Bidding your host *au revoir*, and perhaps meeting some new friends loading up their bikes as well, you pedal to the trail and begin a pleasant, relaxing ride that quickly leaves the village houses behind and splits

a landscape of boreal forest, bubbling brooks, rivers, wetlands, and manicured golf courses. The gradient alternates between hardly uphill and lovingly downhill, so while you do work up a little sweat, you're never slogging forth with any serious effort. Passing other bikers going in the opposite direction, you greet them with a friendly *"Bonjour!"* although they're just as likely to be from Ottawa, Calgary, or even Germany. There are couples, grandparents, students, kids, and occasionally volunteers biking along in case anybody needs any assistance.

It doesn't take long before you meet lovely people enjoying the scenery just as much as you are, like Guy and Julie from Kitchener. You share camera duties, and leave a message scratched in the gravel for Jeff and Katie from Waterloo who can't be too far behind. The trail itself is clearly marked with mileage signs, punctuated every five to ten kilometres with toilets, a shelter, or a small, century-old train station, lovingly restored. At one point a large deer springs out of the trees up ahead. Speedy chipmunks dart in and out of the dense foliage. When you pass through the villages, you'll come across cafés or bistros, the kind of places where the friendly owner takes photos of your group and is so much fun that you ask him to be in the photo as well.

How much biking you decide to do that day is completely up to you — perhaps sixty kilometres, perhaps forty. Your stops are as flexible as your muscles; all you need to do is arrange with the transportation service so that your bags are waiting for you at the next B&B when you arrive. Welcomed by another B&B owner (where do they find these characters?), you lock up your bike for the night, take a warm shower, and enjoy a stroll around the village. There might be a river flowing opposite your B&B, a ceramic arts festival, or a quiet street with cafés and local artists.

Even Granddad Can Do It

In 2011, 54-year-old Winnipeg grandfather Arvid Loewin broke the world record for the fastest bicycle ride across Canada, pedalling 6,055 kilometres from Vancouver to Halifax in just 13 days, 6 hours, and 13 minutes. Spending twenty hours on the saddle each day and averaging just two hours' sleep, Loewin raised hundreds of thousands of dollars for street kids in Kenya. ➤

With four days to accomplish the ride, handily divided into four sections on the easy-to-follow map, chances are you'll arrive at your destination early or mid-afternoon, which leaves you plenty of time to rest before a wonderful gourmet dinner, prepared by an award-winning chef. Your legs are a little tired, and your butt reminds you it's there, but you're also satisfied that you did some exercise today, which helped burn off some of that breakfast! You sleep like a baby.

It's Tuesday morning. Repeat.

Wednesday. Repeat, but your legs and butt are silent.

Thursday, much the same, until you reach Mile Zero in Saint-Jérôme, where your car awaits, parked at the hotel. This is where you were picked up four days ago and driven with your bike to Mont-Laurier, at Mile 230. The week has flown by in a green blur. Your lungs are blossoming with fresh mountain air.

This was my experience biking Quebec's fantastic Le P'tit Train du Nord. It's the beautiful outdoors, with a little exercise, adventure, culture, and the chance to discover the wonders of small-town Quebec. Your bike is waiting.

START HERE: canadianbucketlist.com/traindunord

DISCOVER QUEBEC CITY

"I'm from Europe," jokes comedian Eddie Izzard, "you know, where history comes from." As much history as there is in Canada, there's no denying that a couple of hundred years here — or, in the case of the West, a couple of decades there — doesn't stack up against the centuries of cobblestone that pave the old towns of Europe. *Bienvenue à Quebec City*, a UNESCO World Heritage Site, a pocket of old Europe right here in North America, where history comes from as well.

From the 221-metre-high lookout rotunda atop the Observatoire de la Capitale, I see the stone wall that surrounds the Old Town, the archway of Rue Saint-Jean allowing traffic to pass between the centuries. The fairy-tale turrets of the Château Frontenac loom over sardine-packed old brick buildings like a medieval lord's castle. I see the exact point where the mighty St. Lawrence narrows, an observation that gave birth to the name Quebec itself (which is believed to be an Algonquin word meaning "narrow passage" or "strait"). I see the walls of La Citadelle, a fortress originally built in the 1600s but

QUEBEC

The Château Frontenac

Quebec City's most striking landmark was one of a series of hotels designed by Canadian Pacific Railway to lure tourists onto the rails, and thence into luxurious hotels. Said CPR magnate William Cornelius Van Horne: "If we can't export the scenery, we'll import the tourists!" First came the Banff Springs Hotel (1888) and Château Lake Louise (1890), then New York architect Bruce Price's magnificent Château Frontenac (1893). With its medieval turrets and distinctive copper roofs, the fairy tale–like Château offers sweeping views of the St. Lawrence River. With Quebec City now a National Historic Site, the Fairmont Hotels & Resorts group continues to host guests with luxurious old-world charm. ➤

obtaining its distinctive star shape from British conquerors in the early 1800s. There's the Plains of Abraham, where the French and British battled for what would ultimately be the control of an entire continent. Today, Battlefields Park is a huge recreational area for sport, leisure, and massive festivals in both summer and winter. The impressive Parliament Building towers as parliament buildings often do, while church steeples pierce the sky like the inverted fangs of a vampire. Devoid of billboards and neon lights, I see a view from another place and another time, reminding me of Riga, or Copenhagen, or Paris. Mirroring my experiences in those cities, I head to the streets with no map book, directions, or itinerary of places to see.

Old Quebec City is small enough to walk on foot within a couple of hours, with pockets of interest lying in wait where you least expect them. I stroll down Rue Saint-Louis, which runs directly to Fairmont's grand Château Frontenac, supposedly North America's most photographed hotel. Like Banff Springs and Lake Louise, this former Canadian Pacific Railway hotel inspires feelings of princely grandeur — a contrast to my own hotel, the modern Hilton, that overlooks the old city like a windowed brick. I walk past statues and churches, little shops selling bric-a-brac, Quebec mainstays such as clothing store Simons. Lunch is a quick stop at Chez Ashtons, where they make the cheese curd fresh every day to get that vital poutine squeak.

My walk deposits me in Rue du Petit-Champlain, once the city's slum, now easily among Canada's most beautiful urban walkways.

It's getting a little brisk out, so I warm up with thick hot chocolate with a dash of spice at La Fudgerie. Cheese, wine, baguettes, chocolate — the city practically reeks of the good stuff. There's a crowd gathered at Place-Royale, where Samuel de Champlain founded the continent's first French settlement in 1608. A beautiful mural paints a vivid picture of the city's history since then.

Up the Funiculaire, opened in 1879 and the only one of its kind in North America, I transition to uptown, past the Dufferin Terrace Slide, where I can't help but spend a couple of bucks to race at 70 kilometres an hour on a sled. The adrenalin buzz makes climbing the 310 steps of La Promenade des Gouverneurs a cinch (the views of the St. Lawrence don't hurt either). Lost in thought, I arrive at the Musée national des beaux-arts du Québec, where an old prison has been turned into a wing of the art gallery.

My walk is just a brief introduction, and I relish the opportunity to explore the city further. We have a little bit of Europe here, too, Mr. Izzard. If you haven't already done so, it's well worth adding Quebec City to your bucket list.

Lunenburg, Nova Scotia, and Old San Juan, Puerto Rico, are the only other two urban centres in North America designated as UNESCO World Heritage Sites.

START HERE: canadianbucketlist.com/quebec-city

GO CAVE BASHING IN "THE MAGGIES"

Quebeckers call Îles de la Madeleine — a.k.a. the Magdalen Islands, a.k.a. "The Maggies" — the best-kept secret in the province. An archipelago located in the Gulf of St. Lawrence, each island in the group is surrounded by soft beach in every direction, sporting brightly painted clapboard houses with massive fairway-cut lawns. Atlantic storms shaped this region both physically and culturally. The eroded soft red sandstone cliffs shelter countless sea caves and sentinels, while centuries of Acadian settlers and Anglophone shipwrecks have created a unique bilingual island community. Ancestors of many of the thirteen thousand residents have lived on the island for seven generations, so that surnames are often dispensed with altogether — you are known simply as the son or daughter of your mother or father.

Deep in Quebec, several communities consist of proud Anglos, tracing their lineage to Irish, Scottish, and English shipwrecks. Everyone gets on splendidly.

QUEBEC ↑

The economy of the Maggies is dependent on fishing and tourism. Lobster is a prime catch, gathered during a short six-week season. Tourism is the bigger catch, and mostly Quebecois visitors arrive each summer by plane, ferry, or cruise ship. Blustering wind has also turned the islands into global destination for wind sports, with the shallow lagoons providing ideal conditions for kitesurfing, and endless dune beaches are bang-on for kite buggies. Seafood is abundant — smoked, pickled, grilled, poached — and seal is still on the menu, too. There's a view around every corner, and just one main road connecting the eight major island communities of Havre Aubert, Cap aux Meules, Havre aux Maisons, Grosse Île, Brion, Pointe aux Loups, Île d'Entrée, and Grande Entrée. Well-maintained, brightly painted wooden houses overlooking sandstone cliffs recall the finer aspects of the Atlantic coast, but with an unmistakable Quebecois twist.

For our bucket list, we can choose from:

- A carnival of wind: kitesurfing, kiteboarding, and kite-buggying
- Cycling on the one-hundred-kilometre-long greenbelt that runs across the archipelago
- Sea kayaking along the red cliffs
- Playing with white-coated harp seal pups on an ice floe, the only place in the world where you can do such a thing.

My personal favourite, though — hence the title of this chapter — is cave swimming beneath the sandstone cliffs of Old Harry's Head. *Cave* and *swimming*: two words that don't do the experience any justice.

I'm enjoying a warm breakfast at La Salicorne, a popular *auberge* and restaurant in Grand Entrée that runs sea kayaking and other outdoor excursions. It's September, the tail end of the tourist season, but the best time for wind junkies. Canadian kitesurfing pioneer

QUEBEC

Eric Marchand's Aerosport operation had already introduced me to kite-buggying on the sixteen-kilometre-long Martinique Beach. I was more than happy to let the pilot steer our tandem buggy as it ripped along the sand in twenty-knot winds. Today, grey clouds are spitting rain with an unwelcoming autumn chill, and while I'd much rather cozy up indoors by a fireplace, the bucket list is calling. Thus I find myself squeezing into a seven-millimetre wetsuit under the bemused gaze of a strapping local lass named Sandrine. Joining me is my pal, the well-known hockey writer Lucas Aykroyd, a man of towering height and soothing, modulated voice. Warmed by our thick wetsuits and life jackets, emboldened by the youth of our lovely blue-eyed guide, we reckon we've signed up for a forgettable family-friendly adventure: Hashtag: #weareidiots.

Sandrine drives us to a beach that is being pounded by huge waves. Our instructions are to follow her. She enters the cold water, and veers to the left toward the sandstone cliffs. Lucas and I look at each other with panic in our eyes. "Em … you do see those waves smashing against those cliffs, right?"

"*Oui*, that is cave swimming. Come!" says Sandrine. A swell picks her up, slams her into the rocks, and washes her out again farther down the coast. It looks like one must be an egg short of an omelet to even attempt this, but for some reason waves buttress the swimmer and cushion the blow. Aided by your buoyant protective wetsuit and life jacket, it appears perfectly safe to let the waves smash you against the coastline. At some points, we scale up boulders for some rock jumping; at others, Sandrine instructs us to wait for a big wave to flush us into a cave, and another to flush us out.

"How is it possible for this to be a commercial family excursion?" asks Lucas, shortly after a huge swell spits him out. I'm too busy screaming with fear and elation to care right then. Apparently, local island kids used to do this all the time, and at some point they realized it was safe enough for tourists to do, too.

"Oh, we've had some sprains and bruises, but nothing serious," says Sandrine matter-of-factly. Typically Canadian then: unique,

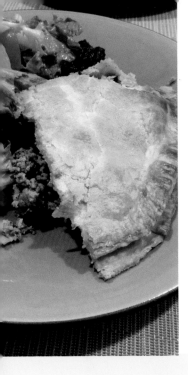

Culinary Quebec

Don't have a taste for fishy-meaty seal salami? You might have better luck with these original Quebecois dishes.

Poutine: The province's gift to world cuisine combines fries, cheese curds, and gravy into an anytime hunger buster.

Tourtière: An anything-goes comfort meat pie, typically made with pork, veal, beef, fish, or wild game.

Tarte au Sucre: My sweetie teethie goodness! Who can turn down a pastry smothered with fudgy sugar and maple syrup?

Soupe aux Pois: Traditional Quebecois pea soup, served thick and hot on cold winter nights.

Pâté Chinois: Although it translates as Chinese Pie, this distinctly non-Asian recipe is very similar to shepherd's pie. ➤

incredible, can't do this anywhere else in world, and you know [shrug] just something we do here for fun.

Two hours later, Lucas and I are deep purple with cold, and not even Sandrine's beaming smile can warm us up. The strong current has pushed us down the coast to a sandy beach, where a guide is waiting with the excursion bus. Later we will toast our courage with a pint of wild herb–scented Belle Saison at the outstanding À l'abri de la Tempête microbrewery. The swells will grow from five to ten, no, eighteen feet — not a word of a lie! We will nosh on dried herring and seal salami at Le Fumoir d'Antan, and artisanal island cheese at Pied-de-Vent. We'll meet friendly locals in clapboard *auberges*, and explore the historic marina of La Grave. Without Sandrine for company, however, we'll skip the long walks on windswept beaches.

Although there are regular flights throughout the summer season from Montreal and Quebec, the Maggies are often overlooked in favour of its more popular maritime neighbours. Yet with an abundance of history, culture, natural beauty, food, and wild adventures, there's nowhere else quite like it. Lucky for you, I never could keep a good secret.

START HERE: canadianbucketlist.com/iles-de-la-madeleine/

FIND MONTREAL'S BEST SMOKED MEAT

When immigrants flooded into Montreal from Europe in the early 1900s, they brought with them passionate quirks and traditional recipes. The Italians delivered their fiery tempers and coffee shops. The Greeks brought their strong family values and their souvlakis. And the Jews? They gave the city a quirky neurosis: world-class delis and bagels that have no equal.

The origin of Montreal's smoked meat sandwiches remains a topic of hot dispute. Some say the recipe is Romanian, others Lithuanian, but there's little point fighting while the food's getting cold. The Montreal smoked meat sandwich is a simple creation of edible perfection: rye bread, thinly sliced. Mustard. A pickle on the side. And the meat: expertly carved, melt-in-your-mouth steamed brisket piled so high you can build a fort with it. Choosing where to enjoy such a dish is no simple matter, and locals will let you know exactly why that is. The Great Smoked Meat Hunt has begun.

It starts at four a.m. at Dunn's, where I wash ashore at this twenty-four-hour deli after a hard night's research in the bars. Here, a brusque, whip-smart server tells me that Dunn's recipe hasn't changed in fifty years, and that, unlike some of the other shops, Dunn's is still "Jewish owned." Not exactly, since the company now has independently owned franchises around the country. The meat

The Bucket List
Smoked Meat Sandwich Tour

Bring a pen, a camera, and one serious appetite. My conscience demands that I warn you not to try this in one day.

1. Schwartz's
2. Lesters
3. The Main
4. Ettingers
5. Smoked Meat Pete's
6. Dunn's
7. Deli Bee's
8. Snowdon Deli

arrives steaming, and melts on my tongue. At four a.m., with food this good, I don't care if Zoroaster Amazonian cross-dressers own Dunn's — the sandwich is sensational.

"Dunn's! You can't go to Dunn's for the real experience!" says the father of a Montreal friend, horrified. So he takes me to Lesters Deli in Outremont, where he advises me to order the hot smoked meat sandwich, medium fat for more flavour. Hasidic wives wheel their babies past our table as I tuck into the sandwich, kosher pickle and a plastic bottle of homemade Montreal spice at the ready. Smoked meat is smoked meat, but under the relieved gaze of a true believer, I confess that Lesters is a mouth-watering notch up from Dunn's.

"Lesters? Are you kidding me!" yells the huge ponytailed bouncer outside a nightclub. He literally grabs me by the collar and pulls me closer. His breath smells of garlic, and his skin like Montreal Old Spice. "Schwartz's. Nothing touches Schwartz's! If you don't go to Schwartz's, I'll . . ." And then he lets me go. At this point, I realize that Montrealers take their smoked meat very, very seriously.

Schwartz's has been Montreal's most famous smoked meat deli (or Charcuterie Hébraïque, as the sign outside says) since 1928. It's inspired a musical, a book, and the interest of Celine Dion,

QUEBEC ↑

who, together with other investors, purchased the business. Big hunks of smoked meat sit in the window, tempting the hungry lineups that gather around mealtimes. The service is curt, the decor basic. I order a takeout sandwich, and since I can't find anywhere to sit, I decide to cruelly eat it across the street, enshrined in food bliss while the salivating eyes of the lineup look on. Oh YES! It's nirvana for the carnivore, a foodgasm of the first order.

I returned the following day, and the next time I was in Montreal, and every time I've been in Montreal since. Schwartz's uses a secret blend of herbs and spices, marinates the meat for ten days, and smokes it without preservatives. It's long resisted the urge to grow and take on the fast-food franchises, which explains why the lines are long. But the wait is worth it.

But I'm not done just yet. Across the street from Schwartz's, close to the bench where I enjoyed my first hit of their smoked meat, is the Main. The meat here is also in the window; there are also dozens of newspaper clippings about the genius of its recipe. By now I've learned about the taste benefits of ordering "old-fashioned" as opposed to the health benefits of ordering "lean." I've debated the origins and recipes of Montreal smoked meat (which writer Mordecai Richler called the "nectar of Judea") and its obvious superiority to smoked meat found in the delis of New York. Who serves the best smoked meat is beside the point. Wherever you end up will deliver the goods, a meaty dream that is infinitely better than any other meat sandwich, anywhere in the world.

START HERE: canadianbucketlist.com/meat

DRINK CARIBOU WITH BONHOMME

Canada has no shortage of feisty public celebrations, but there's only space for a handful on the Bucket List. They don't come any cooler than the Carnaval de Québec. Buried in my pockets, my hands were literally frozen as well. For over half a century, the world's largest winter festival has attracted millions of revellers bundled up for the snow, ice, parades, competitions, activities, and parties. Much like Mardi Gras or Rio's Carnival, the tradition dates back to the Catholic festivals preceding Lent. And like my experience at Mardi Gras and Rio's Carnival, this translates into alcohol and dancing, with the added bonus that both keep you warm.

The Carnaval's official mascot is Bonhomme Carnaval, a jolly snowman with an unnerving smile. He's a cross between Mickey Mouse and Elvis Presley, and his effigy is literally your entrance

QUEBEC

Canada's Best Winter Festivals

A little snow and ice never hurt anyone, and it's sure not going to stop Canadians from getting outdoors and celebrating at our Top 10 Winter Parties.

1. Carnaval de Québec, Quebec City, QC
2. Winterlude, Ottawa, ON
3. Winter Festival of Lights, Niagara Falls, ON
4. Festival du Voyageur, Winnipeg, MB
5. Montreal Highlights Festival, Montreal, QC
6. Yukon Sourdough Rendezvous, Whitehorse, YK
7. Caribou Carnival, Yellowknife, NT
8. Jasper in January, Jasper, AB
9. Toonik Tyme, Iqaluit, NU
10. Telus World Ski and Snowboard Festival, Whistler, BC

ticket into the Carnaval grounds in Quebec City's Battlefields Park. I'm greeted by an ice slide, kids being pulled in sleds, snow sculptures, and deep regret that I didn't add one more layer of underwear. Well, Rio can keep its wild, sweaty street parties, and New Orleans the plastic beads of Fat Tuesday. This seventeen-day Carnaval has dogsledding, snow rafts, hot tubs, human foosball, and an ice palace, complete with ice discos. Over a dozen teams from around the world work through the night on snow sculptures, and all of this can be enjoyed with your cheap entrance ticket.

I head to the top of the hill for an overview. My immediate impression is that the Carnaval site is smaller than I expected, but since the temperature has plummeted to -15°C, perhaps it's wise that the crowds stick close together anyway. Beneath the Ferris wheel, two men in costumes are leading a Zumba class from the palace stage. It's a direct challenge to winter: snow, ice, wind chill? We'll dance to Shakira!

Ice is cracking on my face as the inflatable raft bounces down a bumpy snow channel. Most activities are family friendly, but there's also a fair bit of drinking going on, mostly in the form of caribou, a

hot mulled wine with added whisky. It's perfectly acceptable to buy a Bonhomme staff, twist his head off and fill up the cane with this hot liquor, a welcome and delicious anaesthetic for the cold.

There are daily events taking place during Carnaval, the most popular of which are the float parades and the ice canoe races across the St. Lawrence River. If you need proof that Canadians are a parachute short of a skydive, watch dozens of men and women paddle and run over floating chunks of ice in the St. Lawrence. Sometimes they paddle and run over each other, all for prize money that is small enough for teams to drink in one evening.

Since this is a celebration, I find myself sliding between the ice bars on Grande Allée, a popular evening attraction. Even though snow is piled high on the sidewalks, there's an undeniable spirit permeating the whole city. The *ceinture fléchée*, a traditional French-Canadian

QUEBEC

sash, adds colour to the waists of locals and tourists. Portraits of Bonhomme are everywhere, and while the jolly mascot initially freaked me out with his dead marshmallow eyes, by the end I'm hugging him too, joining small kids bundled up like walking pillowcases.

Canadians live in a northern country where winter is a way of life. Some people deal with it by staying home, others by moving away. Winter Carnaval is correctly revered as one of the world's unique celebrations. If you dress warmly, embrace your inner child, and keep some caribou handy, you won't freeze to death crossing this one off your bucket list.

START HERE: canadianbucketlist.com/carnaval

A Recipe for Caribou

It's easy to make Quebec City's Carnaval drink of choice. Just get your hands on sherry, vodka, brandy, and port. And painkillers for the next morning.

3 oz. (100 mL) vodka

3 oz. (100 mL) brandy

12½ oz. (425 mL) Canadian sherry

12½ oz. (425 mL) Canadian port

Serves 10 (or 7 lushes, 3 bangers, and a partridge in a pear tree)

SNOWMOBILE IN SAGUENAY-LAC-SAINT-JEAN

Large parts of Canada depend on the snowmobile. Since early inventors first strapped skis onto Model T Fords, it's become far more than just a mode of winter transport; it's a way of life.

Quebec claims rightful ownership of this mode of transportation: local boy Joseph Armand-Bombardier invented the caterpillar track, which soon became a vital system for winter ambulances, school buses, and mail and military vehicles. Today, there are more than three million snowmobiles registered worldwide, and Bombardier is a true Canadian success story — whether on water, in the sky, or out on the snow.

That might explain why Quebec boasts a staggering 33,000 kilometres of snowmobile trails. That's enough terrain to overwhelm anyone's bucket list, so we're going to press the throttle to the region of Saguenay Lac-Saint-Jean, which is home to nine snowmobile circuits covering a whopping 3,500 kilometres. Huge amounts of snow fall here every winter, and snowmobilers arrive from around the world to take advantage of it. *Auberges* are polished, bistros are opened, and the trails are groomed and clearly signposted. A seemingly hostile

terrain of deep powder, dense forest, and icy lakes suddenly becomes a playground for powerful machines that roar their approval. It's why riders call this part of the world "Snowmobiler's Paradise."

I sense some of your heads shaking, a thought bubble sprouting: "But I've never been on a snowmobile before. Isn't it dangerous? Don't I need a licence? Aren't they difficult to ride?" *Au contraire.* You don't need a licence to ride a snowmobile. You can go as fast, or as slow, as you want. And danger is often associated with speed and control, and, as with anything — car, bicycle, motorbike, skis — accidents tend to occur when people ride beyond their talent level. Fortunately, snowmobiles are designed to be incredible forgiving. There's a very fast learning curve as you figure out how to shift your weight to take corners more efficiently and keep your ride smooth. In a region that embraces snowmobilers, there are plenty

of gas stations and repair shops if you need them, not to mention friendly camaraderie on the trails. First-timers might want to use the service of a local outfitter like Equinox Adventures, who provide the machines, a guide, a route itinerary, and accommodation for a five-day package. You've heard of ski-in, ski-out lodges. In the part of the world, you sled-in, sled-out.

Quebec's Federation of Snowmobile Clubs charges a trail permit to use their extensive network, primarily to cover the costs of grooming and marking the trails. Online you can find maps with updated conditions to plan your own adventure, or you can choose one of the recommended itineraries (with names like Around the Fjord and the jovially named The Ha! Ha!). Accommodations list which circuit they service, and there are several snowmobile rental shops throughout the region.

Those are the nuts and bolts. But let's get to that moment when you motor up a summit on a blue-sky day. You lift your visor, suck in a mouthful of fresh air, and gaze at a view so extraordinary it revs the horsepower of your heart. Beyond the thrill of gunning a 600 cc machine across a frozen lake or meandering between snow ghosts of trees, lies the fact that snowmobiling is part of Canada's winter DNA. If you get the opportunity to ride one, even for a few hours on a commercial joy ride, you'll quickly understand why.

START HERE: canadianbucketlist.com/saguenay

SWING A SWORD AT TAM-TAMS

During my journey, I'm often struck by how locals might take their gifts for granted. In Newfoundland, icebergs are no bigger a deal than snow-capped mountains are for British Columbians. In Montreal, the fact that thousands of people gather every Sunday in the park for a makeshift celebration as festive as any you'll find on the continent is, you know, Sunday in the park.

In the late 1970s, students began to gather at the base of the Sir George-Étienne Cartier statue in Mount Royal park, bringing their drums, blankets, bicycles, and picnic lunches. Today, all I have to do is walk up Rue Rachel toward the towering angel statue and follow the sound of the beat. *Tam-tam* is the French name for a hand drum, and these drums become the heartbeat of a spontaneous jam session that anyone can join in on — as drummer, dancer, singer, or spectator. Vendors have set up blanket stores around the square selling clothing, fresh fruit, and curios, with the drummers concentrated in one corner, surrounded by a crowd of people. Two beautiful girls

are dancing in the middle (much to the appreciation of the mostly male drummers), and the distinct lack of organization is part of the charm. Somehow the beat builds and climaxes, stopping for enthusiastic applause before resuming in a different direction. This goes on for hours.

Surrounding this energetic rhythm is a familiar park scene: blankets and picnics, people playing cards, doing yoga, reading, kids running about. One bench has a man playing the saxophone, another a family eating ice cream. In the city that gave the world Cirque du Soleil, it's no surprise to see locals practise their juggling, tightrope-walk between trees, and polish their acrobatics. Tattoos and wild steampunk fashions mix with single yuppies, young families, and seniors out for a relaxing stroll — a community nonchalantly doing what it does, so vibrantly and colourfully.

Not far from the drums, I notice a kerfuffle being kicked up in a dust storm. Here I find the medieval foam weaponry fighters, assembled with their foam swords, shields, battle-axes, and blades. Evolving out of the Live Action Role Playing scene of the late 1990s, Sunday battles have become an institution at the park, drawing kids

and adults (of all ages) to chaotic dustdowns. Two fronts assemble organically, and the rules are simple: If you get hit in the chest, you're dead and must leave the field. In the arm or leg, you're immobilized. Two hits and you're dead. Battles last minutes and the hard-core regulars don't stand for cheats. Up to 150 people might gather, including a guild of rather good-looking ladies.

"We don't get an advantage from the guys, so we learn quick," says Lissette, a ten-year veteran, strapping on her knee pads. "Of course, we are known to hit harder."

Anyone can join; just go up and ask some of the regulars hanging out under the trees if you can borrow or rent a weapon. But do be careful. "With my armour, I weigh over four hundred pounds," explains Dominic, a large man holding a much larger lance. "If I fall over, a kid can get hurt." By kid, he means anyone with a penchant for swordplay on sunny afternoons.

I buy an ice cream and wander about with a certain envy in my heart. Although it's legal to drink in public spaces in Quebec, everyone seems considerate and orderly. Few cities would allow such a gathering to take place, not without mountains of red tape, permits, policing, and the fear that things could get out of hand. This is just Montreal in the summer, doing what Montreal does best: celebrating life, even if you can get killed on a dusty battlefield.

START HERE: canadianbucketlist.com/tamtams

SCALE A FROZEN WATERFALL

Canyoning, or canyoneering as it is known in the United States, combines aspects of hiking, climbing, rappelling, and, where applicable, not drowning. The goal is to ascend or descend a canyon, through pristine wilderness like that found around Mont-Sainte-Anne, Quebec. Although relatively obscure, canyoning is a popular activity in the summer, with various routes open to all ages and fitness levels. I've slid down canyons in Costa Rica, where our guide held everyone back so he could "dispose of" a poisonous snake in our path. New Zealand, Colorado, France — the activity isn't unique in itself, but if we return to the winter ski slopes of Mont-Sainte-Anne, we can find something truly original.

Marc Tremblay's Canyoning Quebec is the only place in North America where you can attempt ice canyoning — just the sort of unique activity our bucket list is hungry for. Tall and stringy, Marc is an accomplished spelunker, the kind of guy who gets his rocks off squeaking through caverns underground. He enjoys introducing people to the joys of canyoning and is a pioneer of doing it in snow and ice. He tells me to dress warmly. Drowning is the least of my concerns.

We meet at the ticket office of Mont-Sainte-Anne, where I'm kitted out with ropes, crampons, and a backpack. "The most dangerous things on this trip are crossing the highway and avoiding the snowmobiles," says Marc reassuringly. We hike over to the highway, wait for local drivers hell bent on creating roadkill, and continue along a snowmobile path where Marc's assistant, Genevieve, keeps watch over a blind hill.

Once we enter the woods, we're in a magical world of snow and ice. A stream flows, barely, carving ice structures along its edges. During the summer this path will be full of hikers, but in winter it belongs to us. Farther down, Marc helps me with my crampons, shows me how to loop my figure-eight hook, and ropes me up to practise my descent. "Keep your legs apart, watch out for the crampons and just ease your way down," he instructs me calmly. Child's play, which is why even children can do this. I have to watch my harness, though, which has a tendency to trap testicles, initiating a Michael Jacksonesque falsetto.

We continue downstream until we come to the edge of a forty-metre cascade. In summer, you'd descend down the same spot, showering in the flow of the waterfall. This overcast day in February, I hear water barely descending beneath a spectacular frozen formation. Nature has burned ten thousand giant, icy-white candles, and I'm about to lower myself down among the hardened wax.

Crunch! The sharp teeth of my crampons dig into the ice as I do my best to avoid breaking the frozen stalactites. Once I'm over the lip, I stop to admire the view. Limestone caves would take millennia

to form these sorts of structures, but out here in winter, every day produces a different show. Goosebumps sprout like mushrooms on my neck. I eventually lower myself to the bottom, where Genevieve unhooks me. I greet her with my favourite one-syllable word: "Wow!"

I can barely recognize the waterfall when I see photos taken during the summer, but winter climes offer an entirely different adventure: an icy, exhilarating thrill that belongs on the Central Canada Bucket List.

START HERE: canadianbucketlist.com/canyoning

LAUGH, DANCE, OR LISTEN AT THE GREAT MONTREAL FESTIVALS

Montreal has more festivals than there are weeks in the year: arts, children, music, history, theatre, bikes, fashion, culture — just about everything that tickles your right brain gets the treatment. Other cities—notably Edmonton, Vancouver, Toronto, and Winnipeg — have no shortage of festivals either, so why does Montreal get the nod on the bucket list? Because Montreal does it bigger and sexier than anywhere else.

Take the Montreal International Jazz Festival, the world's largest jazz festival, hosting over one thousand concerts featuring three thousand performers from three dozen countries, attracting some two million people to the city, who visit fifteen concert venues and ten outdoor stages. Remarkably, two-thirds of these performances are completely free of charge, which means everyone has the chance to watch artists such as Prince, Norah Jones, Diana Krall, Ben Harper, and Gilberto Gil perform at the huge outdoor, car-free downtown venues.

Typically scheduled at the end of June, the jazz festival's days get going at the site around eleven a.m., when various events specifically appealing to families begin. Kids can build their own instruments at workshops in the Parc Musical, while bands perform on different stages. It runs all day, until heavyweight performers take the stage, and continues as the crowd filters into the city's legendary late night after-parties. The ten-day event transcends jazz; expect world music, rock, fusion, R&B, folk, and a lineup of virtuosos, all drawn to the event like the thousands they perform for.

Come September, the hipsters gather for Pop Montreal, an indie music festival that took on special significance when local artists Arcade Fire exploded to become one of the world's biggest rock acts. From humble beginnings, the five-day festival has grown to present over six hundred bands in fifty venues and has diversified with an accompanying design festival (Puces Pop), a music conference (Pop Symposium), Film Pop (for film-related music), Art Pop (visual arts),

QUEBEC

and Kids Pop. Montreal's "it" factor draws interest and artists from around the world, and while the festival was only founded in 2002, it has fast become one of the coolest cultural festivals on the continent.

Before seat-back screens allowed a measure of choice, do you remember watching dreary romantic comedies on long-haul flights, if only to alleviate the excruciating boredom? The movie (typically starring Matthew McConaughey's bare chest) would finally end, and filling up the hour would be a timeless episode of the prank series *Just for Laughs Gags*. Suddenly, hundreds of people of ridiculously diverse backgrounds were cracking up in unison at the situations — all created, produced, and executed to perfection in Montreal. Humour transcends language.

So it's fitting that every July, Montreal hosts Just for Laughs, the world's largest international comedy festival. It's more than just stand-up from the world's funniest French and English comedians. The event turns the streets of downtown Montreal into a festival, with parades, food trucks, and packed pedestrian-only promenades. Meanwhile, TV execs and producers hunt for the next breakout comedy star. You may have heard of some of them: Jerry Seinfeld, Chris Rock, Tim Allen, Jay Leno, Jim Carrey. Rowan Atkinson did his first non-verbal Mr. Bean performance in front of an audience at Just for Laughs. I ask a cheerful Gilbert Rozon, who founded the event back in 1983, how Montreal has somehow become the funniest place on earth.

"In Quebec, we have a beautiful expression, 'C'est le fun!' It should be our national slogan, and it's typical about Montreal," he tells me. "Nobody can be against being happy, nobody ever said 'I laughed too much.'" Gilbert reflects on Montreal's legacy as a party town during Prohibition, how it attracted crooners from the 1930s to the 1960s, and how the current festivals uniquely close the streets and offer so many free shows.

Led by its own iconic green Bonhomme, Just for Laughs features comedy theatre, music, dance, and other types of performances. North America's best stand-up stars host gala evenings, usually televised around the world. Outside the theatres, crowds flock to the pedestrian-only Ste-Catherine Street, enjoying the free spectacle under the lights in the Quartier des Spectacles, which reminds me of the Sambadromo in Rio. Call it a carnival of comedy.

"In the next thirty years, we're going to invest in beauty, and build more events around this time, so that you'll have no choice but to want to visit," says Gilbert, like a generous kid who wants to share his candy.

Later that evening, I join the long lineup to see a festival staple: the Nasty Show. Renowned for the vulgarity of its stand-ups — the show's run has featured greats such as Bill Hicks and Denis Leary — tonight's performance is a shotgun of hysterical bad taste. Before you push up daisies, visit Montreal one summer to laugh so hard the tears streak down your face.

START HERE: canadianbucketlist.com/festivals

SURF A STANDING WAVE
(IN A MAJOR CITY)

The first time I tried surfing, some bleached beach bums gave me a small board best suited for experts and towed me into a shark-infested meat grinder affectionately known as the Snake Pit. This was in the warm Indian Ocean off the east coast of South Africa. The fangs of the waves repeatedly bit, while the tail of backwash coiled around and sucked the life out of me. Fortunately, the sharks weren't biting that day.

With an introduction like that, it's no wonder that I still can't get up on a surfboard, although I have tried in other, less hostile environments. There's a draw about surfing that is hard to hang ten on … a curious blend of nature and exhilaration, patience and full blown action. It's why people of all ages and interests become hooked, and why it belongs on our bucket list. There's just one problem: we live in the Great White North.

What Canadian surf lacks in weather and waves, it make up with creativity. Advances in wetsuit technology make the cold swells of B.C.'s Tofino and Nova Scotia's Lawrencetown manageable, while Lake Superior's north shore kicks up encouraging surf in spots like Stoney Point and Park Point.

Those seeking a consistent wave close to the amenities of a major urban city need look no further than Habitat-67. Located close to the iconic building of the same name, the St Lawrence's Lachine rapids reach as high as two metres, creating one of the world's largest standing waves. These are especially fun to learn on, since you can spend more time learning how to balance on the board, and less time waiting for the right wave to come along and throw you off it. If you don't know where to start, hang in there, dude. KSF, located right by the rapids, is a full service surf shop offering gear rentals, instruction classes, and stand-up paddle-boarding. No snakes, no sharks, just stoke.

START HERE: canadianbucketlist.com/habitat67

SPEND A NIGHT IN AN ICE HOTEL

Five hundred tons of ice, fifteen thousand tons of snow, thirty-six rooms, and one travel writer desperately trying to avoid using the word *cool*. The Hôtel de Glace, located outside Quebec City, is North America's only ice hotel. It takes fifty people about six weeks to build the hotel each winter, crafting its rooms, bar, chapel, passageways, slides, and chandeliers. Lit with atmospheric non-heat-emitting LED lights, you'll get plenty of ambience if not warmth standing next to the double-glazed fireplaces. Not to fear, the romance and creative vision of the hotel will warm your heart just as surely as the interior temperature of -5°C will chill your bones.

At around nine p.m., day visitors are ushered out and the over-night guests gather in the Celsius, an adjacent, blessedly heated building, for the briefing. If you're going to spend the night in a Popsicle, the goal is not to become one in the morning. All guests are required to sit through a training session.

"The two most important things I can tell you," explains our bilingual, dreadlocked guide, "is don't go to sleep cold, and under no circumstances go to sleep wet." Put your glasses on the bedside table (made of ice) and they will soon be part of the installation. Spending the night in a hotel made of snow and ice requires a rather adventurous guest. It becomes clear that those seeking luxury and comfort will prefer your run-of-the-mill thawed hotel.

All guests are assigned lockers in the Celsius, where you'll also find bathrooms and showers. Nothing goes into your room except your pyjamas, boots and outdoor jacket. And while the builders have invented ice glasses to serve chilled vodka cocktails, they haven't invented ice plumbing, so no, there are no toilets in the ice hotel. Each bed sits on a piece of wood atop blocks of ice, with a carved ice headboard and striking sculptures in the 1.2-metre-thick walls. We are shown how to wrap ourselves in our cocoon sleeping bags, which are designed for -30°C conditions and therefore should have no problem keeping us warm at night.

Your Bed for the Night

Each bed has a solid ice base, with a wooden bedspring and mattress on top, covered with blankets. Guests are provided with Arctic sleeping bags and isolating bedsheets that can keep you toasty up to -30°C. It is recommended you sleep in thermal, moisture-wicking underwear, as moisture generated by body heat will likely trap and freeze. No matter how cold it is outside, the rooms stay between -3°C and -5°C. Warm yourself up in the hot tub or sauna before you turn in, and try not to think about the bathroom in the middle of the night! ➤

Slide into the bag liner and then into the bag itself, blow out the candles and turn off the glow lights with the switch cleverly built directly into your ice bed. Couples expecting a hot, passionate night in their Winter Wonderland are in for a disappointment. Exposed skin is simply not a good idea, and the sleeping bags are designed for a snug, solo fit. Although, this being Quebec, a province of passion, the designers merely ask that you get creative. How else to explain the naked life-sized couple staring at my bed? Or the hands grafted onto the headboard suggesting a night of icy consummation? Perhaps there's a connection between hot thoughts and body warmth.

Before bedtime, there's plenty of time to explore the large public areas. Music thumps in the ice bar, where four hundred people can gather to drink and dance, and you never have to ask the friendly bartenders for ice in your cocktails. The chapel hosts dozens of weddings each year, with guests sitting on benches covered in deerskin while the doors are covered in fur. There's a room explaining the annual theme, sponsor exhibits, slides for adults and kids, and the fresh smell of ozone in the air.

Overnight guests are encouraged to hit the hot tubs and dry sauna before they go to sleep, warming up the body for the night ahead. I arrived after the Celsius kitchen had closed, so the attendant at the front desk, staffed twenty-four hours a day, ordered me a pizza. I half expected it to arrive in a frozen box.

Light snow is falling when I leave the hot tub, shower, put on my thermal underwear, and get ready for the night ahead. Please, please, please don't let me need to pee in the middle of the night!

Everything is locked up, making it exceptionally easy for guests to vacate by 8:30 a.m., staff to collect sleeping bags, and the rooms to open for public viewing tours by 9:30. No housekeeping is required, other than raking the floor and straightening out the fur covers on the bed and benches.

The hotel has been built, and rebuilt each year, since 2001, and is open from the first week of January until the last week of March. Lying in the deep silence and darkness of my room, I wonder if the builders and designers are heartbroken to watch their efforts melt each spring. Or perhaps they're excited at the potential to start afresh next season? How many other hotels can literally reconfigure themselves each year? Watching the vapour of my breath, I lie awake, wide-eyed and aware of just how unique this experience is.

Ninety-nine percent of overnight guests stay just one night. Dress warmly and prepare for an adventure. One night in one of the world's most unusual hotels is all our Bucket List is asking for.

START HERE: canadianbucketlist.com/icehotel

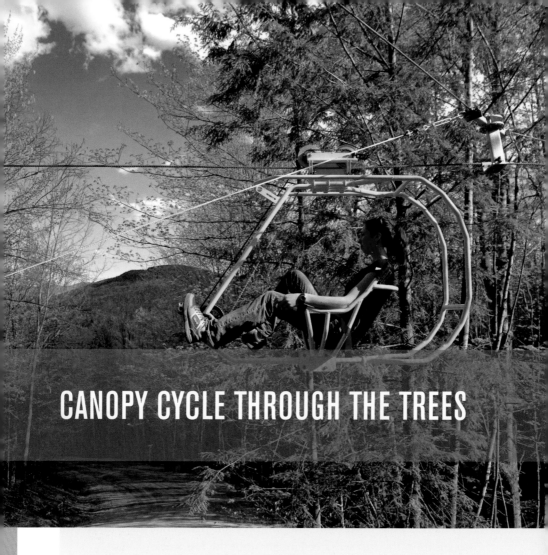

CANOPY CYCLE THROUGH THE TREES

Bucket lists are all about doing things you've never done before. And while hiking, mountain biking, and ziplining are all worthy outdoor pursuits, you can do them in lots of places. Hang on … what if we could do them all at the same time?

Just a ninety-minute drive from Montreal, near the town of Sutton, is a four-season outdoor resort called Au Diable Vert. Its tree house accommodations are pretty neat, as are its hiking and ski trails, water activities, and shaggy Highland cows. But we're here, however, for a peculiar contraption they call the VéloVolant. Welcome to the world's highest suspended bicycle ride.

A Bucket List Full of Edible Delights

Foodies, take note: Charlevoix, a region long known for the quality of its meats, cheeses, desserts, vegetables, and fruits, now has its own Flavour Trail. More than forty producers, farmers, and restaurateurs have banded together to showcase the finest products of region, with a loop starting at Petite-Rivière Saint-François and ending at La Malbaie. Join farmers for tours of the fields, sit down in the finest restaurants, browse local markets, or pick up some warm bread, cold cider, and unripened cheese for a picnic. You'll find a handy guide with recommendations and routes online. ➤

Although the line is relatively flat and stays at the same level, the ground disappears beneath your feet once you pedal off the platform, and you'll soon be hovering thirty metres above the ground. Seated and safely strapped in, you'll pass over maple and pine forests, ravines, and waterfalls, listening to birdsong, perhaps encountering some wildlife foraging below. Fifteen riders are spaced out along the one-kilometre circuit, which takes about forty-five minutes to complete. While you can pedal faster to gain some speed, think less zipline or roller coaster and more a gentle cycle in the forest. A first in Canada, our bucket list applauds the impressive efforts of whomever keeps coming up with these increasingly bizarre methods to enjoy our great outdoors.

START HERE: canadianbucketlist.com/velo

ENJOY POUTINE, WITH FOIE GRAS

Canada has gifted the world gourmet treats well above its station, and any self-respecting bucket list should include a sample of the staples. I'm talking about ginger ale, instant mash, processed cheese, Timbits, and Yukon Gold potatoes fried in canola oil. Back bacon boosts a breakfast, Beaver Tails sweeten up cold days, and maple sugar is our apple pie (and goes great with apple pie, too).

If I were to choose a single Canadian dish that could take over the world, it would be poutine. It takes fries, a universally loved food group served from bistros to trucker bars, and simply makes them better. Poutine — healer for the hangover, sweet gravied taters for the stomach's soul. To foreigners, adding cheese curds and gravy to fries might sound as appetizing as adding clams to tomato juice, but Canadians know how a little creativity can raise the bar.

While several Québécois communities claim its invention, and the word itself has been around for ages, poutine only became popular in the late 1960s. In Quebec City, I was directed to Chez Ashton, a franchise that built its fame on the sloppy back of poutine as far back as 1972. Greasy as the greasiest spoon, one bite of their hand-cut potatoes smothered in brown gravy and the day's freshly made squeaky cheese curds was better than any poutine I've tried on the west coast. Served in a foil container it may be, but still fit for a king.

Montreal's La Banquise offers twenty-eight varieties of poutine, including La Elvis (ground beef, green peppers, mushrooms), La Kamikaze (spicy sausages, hot peppers, and Tabasco) and La Obélix (smoked meat). Poutine's beauty is that you can't really go wrong with it, but for our Bucket List we're off to Montreal's hip Plateau neighbourhood, and a restaurant called Au Pied de Cochon. Celebrity chef Martin Picard is known for his creativity and, as Anthony Bourdain calls it, his "porky and ducky" decadence.

Seated next to me at the bar overlooking the open-concept kitchen are two guys: a bureaucrat who timed his Montreal connection to Ottawa specifically to visit the restaurant, and a bartender from Toronto who plans his trips to Montreal around available reservations. Booking is a must, at least a month ahead for large groups, a week for couples. An attractive server walks past with a cooked pig's head on a platter with a large lobster in its mouth. Behind me, a woman is chewing on a bison rib as long as my forearm. I scan the menu: fresh seafood, handily divided into bivalve, gastropod, echinoderm, cephalopod, and crustacean sections. Pickled tongue. Foie gras hamburger. Duck carpaccio. And there it is: foie gras poutine, calling me like three angels playing heavy metal on their harps.

QUEBEC

Canada's Culinary Contribution

Poutine is not the only edible gift Canada has given the world:

1. **Butter tarts:** The sugar-syrup-egg-and-butter delight was once a staple of pioneer cooking.
2. **Nanaimo bars:** A chocolate-custard-wafer sandwich invented on Vancouver Island.
3. **Tourtière:** Crispy spiced meat pie, typically served at Christmas, but delicious year-round.
4. **Beaver Tails:** The name of Ottawa's hot sugared pastry continues to confound international tourists.
5. **Fricot:** A hearty Acadian meat stew enjoyed when times were tough, and enjoyed when they weren't.
6. **McIntosh:** The crunchy, tart apple discovered by Mr. McIntosh on his farm in Upper Canada back in 1811 provides Americans with the main ingredient for their finest apple pies and was the inspiration for the name of Apple Inc.'s Mac computers.
7. **Maple syrup:** Canada produces 85 percent of the world's favourite syrup, which works on everything from pancakes to salmon.
8. **Fish and brewis:** Codfish + hard bread + salted pork fat = Newfoundland's comfort food. ➤

Foie gras is, of course, a controversial food group, but wise travellers should respect local customs. David, the bureaucrat, orders Duck in a Can, which is so rich and fabulous he breaks out into a joyous sweat, calling it Heart Attack in a Can. Rare duck breast cooked with foie gras and vegetables, marinated in balsamic vinegar, opened and plopped onto mashed potatoes richer than butter. Paul the bartender orders a buckwheat pancake with bacon, mashed potatoes, foie gras, and maple syrup from Picard's popular sugar shack. "It's little, but it hits you hard," says Paul, twitching from the excess.

My poutine arrives smothered in a thick gravy, the chips fried in duck fat (of course), with a slab of sinful foie gras on the top. The aroma contains enough calories to feed a village in North Korea. It tastes like winning the jackpot on the first pull of a slot machine, and contains the Higgs boson particle of flavour. Another guy at the bar has ordered the same, and while he doesn't say much, his face turns the ruby shade of beet. Our friendly, attractive servers have mischievous glints in their eyes. They've seen it all before, and they'll see it all again. "Are you enjoying your meal?" they ask.

"It's . . . to die for," I answer.

START HERE: canadianbucketlist.com/poutine

TAP A TREE FOR MAPLE SYRUP

Quebec has dozens of sugar shacks open to the public, and visiting at least one of them in early spring definitely belongs on the bucket list. So how exactly does one tap a tree?

1. Choose a healthy-looking maple tree at least twelve inches in diameter, exposed to lots of direct sunlight.
2. Bring a bucket, spile, mallet, and a drill with a 5/16 or 7/16 drill bit.
3. Tap on the south side of the tree (which gets the most sunlight), preferably below a large branch or above a root. Make sure you're at least six inches away from any previous tapping holes.
4. Drill your hole at a slight angle to make the sap flow downward. Remove all shavings.
5. Use your mallet to gently tap in the spile, careful not to split the wood.
6. Hang your bucket on the edge of the spile, making sure it is stable and won't blow over or fall. Cover it to prevent dirt and bugs getting to the sap.

7. Collect your sap in the afternoons. If the temperature rises to above 7°C, stick it in the fridge so it doesn't spoil.
8. Sap generally flows for four to six weeks, with the best sap collected at the start of the flow.

Depending on conditions, a healthy tree can provide between thirty-seven and three hundred litres of sap during a season. The sap is then boiled and strained to make pure maple sugar or syrup. For recommended sugar shacks and recipes:

START HERE: canadianbucketlist.com/maple

SCALE THE VIA FERRATA AT MONT-TREMBLANT

Several years ago I found myself atop a holy mountain in central China, standing on two narrow wooden planks leaning against a wall of solid vertical rock. Below me was a thousand-metre drop. Trust me when I say I was ill-prepared for this experience, as many others had been before me. To prevent people inconveniently falling off and dying, Chinese authorities insist all visitors to Mount Hua pay a few bucks for a harness to clip into a static safety line running the length of the "Number One Cliffside Plank Path."

This was my introduction to the exciting world of the via ferrata (Italian for "iron road"), a fun adventure for those of us who want to climb mountains without having to risk actually climbing a mountain. Popular in Europe, there are but a few via ferratas in Canada. The largest is Mount Nimbus, accessible only by helicopter near Golden, B.C.

There are others near Whistler, Gatineau, Quebec City, and Saguenay, but among the most popular and spectacular is the via ferrata in Quebec's largest and oldest national park, Mont-Tremblant, adjacent to the popular ski resort, located 130 kilometres from Montreal.

I drive into the park on a smooth blacktop road that bends and curves through thick boreal forest, a fun roller coaster in itself. It's mid-morning when I get to the park kiosk, signing a waiver in return for a climbing harness, lanyards, helmet, and carabiners. Groups are limited to eight, with the one-kilometre trail divided into three levels of difficulty. I felt bold enough to select the advanced trail, which typically takes about five hours. Sure, one kilometre is no biggie when you're walking on land, but when you have to clip and unclip your way forward against a vertical wall on iron staples with a two-hundred-metre drop beneath your feet, well, it pays to take your time. Our guide, Valérie, shows us how to easily lock into the iron rungs and steel safety line, and

QUEBEC

119

we start off with an imposing suspension bridge over the Diable River. Apparently this is enough to make some people turn back, but here's the surefire Esrock Method for Dealing with These Things:

1. Don't Panic.
2. Trust Your Gear.
3. Remind Yourself You're in Canada, not China, and Things Usually Work in Canada.

Jump "The Rock"

Some people like climbing rocks, others prefer jumping off them. At sixty-one metres high, Great Canadian Bungee's "The Rock" is the highest bungee jump in North America. Overlooking a spring-fed lagoon in Wakefield, Quebec (about a half-hour drive from Ottawa), the rebound alone is higher than any other jump on the continent. Drench yourself in adrenalin by requesting a water dip. Three, Two, One …

START HERE: canadianbucketlist.com/bungee ➤

Designed by conservationists to minimize damage to the environment but overdo the safety aspect for visitors, the line and rungs make their way along the cliff, getting more and more difficult as we progress. Slowly I get used to clipping in every few metres. Always make sure at least one of your carabiners is locked in and it's pretty much impossible to fall more than a couple of feet. I'd say the rest is literally child's play, although kids under fourteen have to turn back before reaching the advanced level.

Here things take a puckering turn as the path moves horizontally against a solid cliff face, the glorious view of the Laurentians and surrounding valley on full display. Standing on an iron rung nailed into the rock, I take my time, breathing it all in — the forest, meandering brown river, the ski slopes visible on the highest peaks. *C'est le fun!* Farther along is a "surprise," in the form of a narrow wooden beam perilously positioned in a crevice. Next is a tightrope bridge, where the braver among the group let go to just hang around in their harness, enjoying the experience of being fully exposed to the elements. Climbers know it's one thing to hike up a mountain shaded by the trees and another to ascend from the outside, hugging solid rock. If the weather isn't great, you may get lashed with wind and rain, but the view accompanies you all the way to the top.

While it's not for everyone (particularly anyone with a fear of heights, or weight or fitness issues), I will say this: In China, I recorded a little video about my experience, which has been seen over one million times on YouTube. This devilish, little-known via ferrata in Mont-Tremblant might not be as exotic, but it's just as thrilling an adventure.

START HERE: canadianbucketlist.com/tremblant

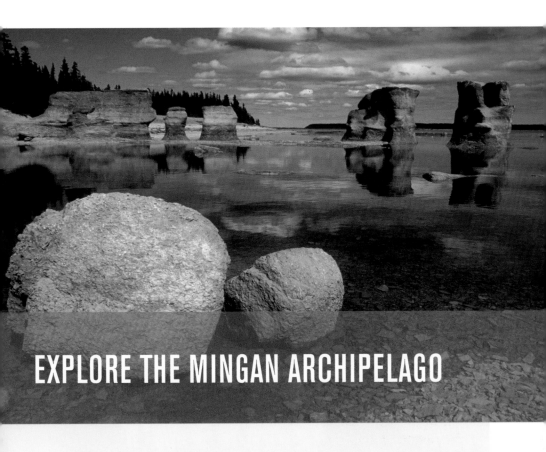

EXPLORE THE MINGAN ARCHIPELAGO

Five hundred million years ago, a warm tropical sea covered what is today the St. Lawrence Lowlands. It would have been swell to relax on its beach, although good luck finding poutine, cheese, or even potatoes for that matter. Over the course of millions of years, fossils, sediment and seabed became compressed into rock, which was then exposed when the sea receded, ready to be carved and eroded by ice-age glaciers, wind, rain, rivers and waves. Take a time-machine forward to the present day and you can find the largest concentration of erosion monoliths in the country.

Almost one thousand islands and islets lay scattered east to west across 150 kilometres of Quebec coastline, moulded into over-hangs, caves, arches, flowerpots, and cliffs. Protected as the Mingan Archipelago National Park Reserve, the area is accessible via boat tours from the north shore of the Gulf of St. Lawrence, from towns such as Longue-Pointe-de-Mingan, Aguanish, and Havre-Saint- Pierre. The

boats vary in terms of their size and destinations, but typically visit several of the more dramatic islands, with park interpreters explaining the festooned cliffs, fossils, tidal pools, and the area's unique geological history. It is possible to camp in the archipelago (taxi boats will shuttle you back and forth from the mainland). You can even find sandy beaches. Having experienced my personal island paradise in the Philippines and Thailand, at least I no longer have to go all the way to Asia.

Another option is a week-long kayaking trip, paddling between the rock giants and beaching on the flats at low tide. With some two hundred species of birds in the park, birdwatchers will enjoy a visit in spring, when marine birds including puffins, guillemots, and kittiwakes build nesting colonies. Alternatively, the summer months bring terns, shorebirds, and sea ducks migrating for food.

Highlights on the western islands are Île aux Perroquets, with its century-old lighthouse buildings, and the treeless Île Nue de Mingan, with its Arctic and subarctic microclimate. The archipelago's largest islands are located in the central sector, accessible from Havre-Saint-Pierre. Île Niapiskau and Île Quarry have the park's most prominent and striking monoliths, with a popular trail across the reef flats of Île du Fantôme and wild festooned cliffs farther east on Île de la Fausse Passe.

Located a ten-hour drive from Quebec City, the otherworldly landscapes of Mingan fall somewhat under the radar. One more reason to add them to the Great Central Canada Bucket List.

START HERE: canadianbucketlist.com/mingan

My bucket list began with an accident. A car ran a stop sign in downtown Vancouver, plowed into my bike, and broke my kneecap. It was just the sort of brush with death one needs to remind oneself of the importance of living. I quit my job, cashed in a $20,000 insurance settlement, bought a round-the-world ticket, and set out to tick off my bucket list. Twelve months and twenty-four countries later, I returned home with the realization that bucket lists grow and evolve like the rest of us. Ten years later, I'm still writing new ones. Like a game of whack-a-mole, if you tick one item off at the top, another pops up at the bottom. This proved especially true when I set out to explore the vastness of Canada.

People we meet create the paradise we find, and it is they who shade the colours of our journey. My single biggest piece of advice for any of these experiences: share them with people you like, and if you're on your own, be open and friendly to those around you. Travelling is as personal as the wear and tear on your toothbrush. You might not meet the folks I met, have the same weather, or enjoy each experience as much as I did, but how you end up exploring Central Canada will ultimately be as unique as you are, even if it's only by reading the pages of this book.

While *The Great Central Canada Bucket List* introduced a variety of experiences, I'm well aware there are woeful omissions, places and adventures known and less-known that I haven't got to just yet. Visit canadianbucketlist.com, and feel free to let me know what they are. I expect this bucket list will keep growing over the years, because the more we dig, the more we'll find, and the more we find, the more we can share with locals and visitors alike.

Charlevoix, Manitoulin Island, the Eastern Townships, the Toronto International Film Festival, surfing Habitat 67, the Elora

Gorge, the New France Festival, one-of-a-kind restaurants and hotels — there's always more to discover. Every chapter in this book concludes with two important words: **START HERE**. I'll end the book with two more: **START NOW**.

RE
robin@robinesrock.com
@robinesrock

ACKNOWLEDGEMENTS

This Bucket List is the result of many miles and many hours of travel, with the professional and personal help of many people and organizations. My deep gratitude to all below, along with all the airlines, ferries, trains, buses, hotels, B&B's, and organizations who helped along the way.

ONTARIO: Ontario Tourism Marketing Partnership, Jantine Van Kregten, Kattrin Sieber, Vanessa Somarriba, Ann Swerdfager, Melanie Wade, Melanie Coates, Michael Braham, Henriette Riegel, Irene Knight, Sue Mallabon, Niagara Parks, the Toronto Maple Leafs, Paul Pepe, Ian McMillan, Cathy Presenger, Larry Lage, Steve Kristjanson, Helen Lovekin, John Langford, Matt Rothwell.

QUEBEC: Tourisme Québec, Gillian Hall, Patrick Lemaire, Paule Bergeron, Magalie Boutin, Catherine Binette, Pierre Bessette, Gilbert Rozon, Lola Burke, Lucas Aykroyd, Suzie Loiselle, everyone who joined me for Carnaval and on the Via Ferrata.

SPECIAL THANKS: David Rock, Karen McMullin, Margaret Bryant, Kirk Howard, Carrie Gleason, Allison Hirst, Synora van Drine, Courtney Horner, Hilary McMahon, Cathy Hirst, Jon Rothbart, Elyse Mailhot, Ian Mackenzie, Sean Aiken, Gary Kalmek, Joe Kalmek, Heather Taylor, Guy Theriault, Jennifer Burnell, Lauren More, Joshua Norton, Ann Campbell, Linda Bates, Patrick Crean, Gloria Loree, Ernst Flach, The Canadian Tourism Commission, Go Media Marketplace, Josephine Wasch, Ken Hegan, Jarrod Levitan, Vancouver and Burnaby Public Libraries, Zebunnisa Mirza, Melissa Morra, Chris Lee, Sherill Sirrs, Marc Telio, Brandon Furyk, Mary Rostad, RtCamp, and the Kalmek and Esrock families.

SPECIAL THANKS TO THE FOLLOWING, WITHOUT WHOM THERE WOULD BE NO COMPANION WEBSITE OR SPEAKING TOURS:

Ford Canada, Parks Canada, VIA Rail, Travel Manitoba, Tourism Saskatchewan, Tourism New Brunswick, Destination BC, Tourism Prince Edward Island, World Expeditions, and Keen Footwear.

And finally, to my parents, Joe and Cheryl Kalmek (without whom there would be no Robin Esrock), my ever-supportive wife, Ana Carolina, and my daughter, Raquel Ayla: *Yay! Aipane! Uppee!*

PHOTO CREDITS

The Great Atlantic Canada Bucket List

Most Canadians think of travel as a way to escape the snow, cold, and dreary winter skies. But Robin Esrock loves all that our eastern provinces have to offer, and so will you! *The Great Atlantic Canada Bucket List* highlights the best travel experiences to be had on Canada's East Coast.

Not your typical travel guide, Robin's recommendations encompass outdoor adventure and natural wonders as well as the unique food, culture, and history of the Maritimes.

Categorized by province, *The Great Atlantic Canada Bucket List* will give you a first-hand perspective on:

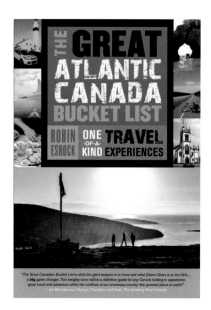

- Ziplining over a waterfall in New Brunswick.
- Harvesting an iceberg for a Newfoundland cocktail.
- Exploring Nova Scotia's Cabot Trail.
- Walking the seabed beneath Hopewell Rocks.
- Cycling across Prince Edward Island.
- Rafting a tidal wave in the Bay of Fundy.
- and much more!

The Great Canadian Bucket List

With a career that has spanned the world, Robin Esrock was amazed at the wealth of unmissable experiences in Canada — and you will be, too.

On his personal quest to check off the best of his home country, travel writer and host Robin Esrock catalogues must-sees, including nature, food, culture, history, adrenaline rushes, and quirky Canadiana. After spending years crafting the definitive Canadian Bucket List, he's packed in enough for a lifetime, at least.

A few of the highlights include:

- Ziplining over a giant waterfall in New Brunswick.
- Digging for dinosaur bones in Alberta's badlands.
- Harvesting an iceberg to make a refreshing Newfoundland cocktail.
- Floating in Canada's own Dead Sea.
- Cracking a Canadian Da Vinci Code in Winnipeg.
- Hiking the tundra under Nunavut's midnight sun.

The companion website presents extensive bonus content: on-the-ground info, videos, gear guides, hotel and tour recommendations, and more. Join the community of Bucket Listers sharing their experiences as they follow Robin's trail.

COMING IN WINTER 2016

The Great Northern Canada Bucket List

Having travelled to over one hundred countries on six continents, international travel guru and bestselling author Robin Esrock turns his attention to Canada's three northern territories. Robin set out to personally tick off the one-of-a-kind destinations and activities you must, and can only do, in the Yukon, Northwest Territories, and Nunavut. He never expected such a range of experiences, and neither will you:

- Dogsledding with a Yukon Quest legend.
- Watching the Northern Lights.
- Camping on an ice floe.
- Drinking the world's most revolting cocktail.
- Hiking Canada's largest national park.
- Rafting the Nahanni River.
- Flying with the world's only DC-3 airline.

The Great Canadian Prairies Bucket List

In *The Great Canadian Prairies Bucket List*, bestselling author Robin Esrock turns his attention to the Canadian prairies. Robin spent years personally finding these one-of-a-kind destinations and activities that you absolutely have to do in Manitoba and Saskatchewan:

- Floating in Canada's Dead Sea.
- Tracking polar bears alongside Hudson Bay.
- Horseback riding with free-roaming bison.
- Discovering ancient archaeological mysteries in Winnipeg.
- Learning what it takes to join the RCMP.
- Attending the largest gathering of snakes in the world.
- Cheering with the wildest sports fan in Canada.
- Lazing on a tropical beach on a prairie lake.

Together with an extensive up-to-date companion website, Robin provides all the inspiration and information you'll need to follow in his footsteps.

VISIT US AT

Dundurn.com
@dundurnpress
Facebook.com/dundurnpress
Pinterest.com/dundurnpress